The Life Of The Venerable Benedict Joseph Labre [by G. L. Marconi]. Tr. [by J. Barnard]. Together With An Appendix, Giving An A Ccount Of Several Miracles

Giuseppe Loreto Marconi, Benoît Joseph Labre (st.)

Miracles of St. Stephen - 173-176
  General Confession - 82
  "visit the body of St James" - 83
  St. Francis - 85
  On the merit of pilgrimages - 87, 88
  Shoes - 90
  ate only scraps - 92
  "continual prayer" - 91, 94, 89

[T]his blessed man (BJL) ... incessantly works miracles in favor of those who with faith invoke his intercession. ... From the time of his death (April 16, 1783) to his day (May 1, 1783), they reckon up to sixty three miracles of the first magnitude." - 189 - 191

"[T]his voluntarily poor man always went to the Churches where the ... Forty Hours' prayer was held." - 186

knees" - 94, 95, 106, 101,
  rags" - 106
he embraced with a cordial affection, all the humiliations which accompany
  life of poverty and penance." ... - 106
he led a life of the greatest self-denial " - 104
Blessed are the Poor in Spirit" - 93
great was his humility" - 98
[He] made a great number of ejaculatory prayers. ... he was almost every moment of s time employed in prayer, and made it his continual occupation. ... meditation
  the sufferings of our Divine Redeemer - 101, 100, 103
lence - 103, 104

J. Barlow fecit London.

BENEDICT JOSEPH LABRE.

THE
LIFE
OF THE VENERABLE

BENEDICT JOSEPH LABRE,

WHO DIED AT ROME,

IN THE

ODOUR OF SANCTITY,

ON THE SIXTEENTH OF APRIL, 1783.

TRANSLATED

FROM THE FRENCH.

TOGETHER WITH AN

APPENDIX,

Giving an Account of feveral Miracles, faid to have been wrought by his Interceffion: foon after his Death.

Juftum deduxit Dominus per vias rectas, et oftendit illi regnum Dei, et dedit illi fcientiam fanctorum, honeftavit illum in laboribus, et complevit labores illius. Sap. x. 10.

WIGAN:

Printed by WILLIAM BANCKS.

MDCCLXXXVI.

THE
CONTENTS.

THE

THE

AUTHOR'S PREFACE,

PREFIXED TO THE

ITALIAN EDITION.

ALMIGHTY GOD, *who alone doth wonderful things, who raiſeth up the needy from the duſt, and lifteth up the poor from the dunghill, that he may ſit with the Princes, and hold the throne of glory:* has vouchſafed in our days to raiſe up a poor man, who was born in France, and known by the name of *Benedict Joſeph Labre,* and in proportion to the obſcurity of his life, has rendered him ſo much more illuſtrious after his death. And, as we piouſly believe, has put him in poſſeſſion of that bleſſed kingdom promiſed to the poor *in ſpirit:* as a proof of which he

7   b   exerts

exerts the power of his right hand, and renews his prodigies.

All Italy has been already surprized and astonished: and the wonderful works, which are said to be wrought every day not only in Rome, but also in very distant places, are more manifest, and more astonishing than his extraordinary virtues, which his most profound humility always made him extremly industrious to conceal. In consequence of such a number of surprizing events, which happened immediately after his death, there arose in all people a natural desire of knowing what kind of man this was, by whom God was pleased to work so many wonders: and what were the qualities and virtues with which he had been adorned. Which beginning to be rumoured about; some officious persons (I know not out of what motive) have set themselves about printing several things concerning him, partly from common report, partly from mere imagination, and some that were even manifestly false. And some others have

have done the fame in fome diftant places.

It was therefore wifely refolved by the Superiors here in Rome, to forbid the publication of fuch uncertain and falfe accounts : and to order that a true and faithful hiftory, of his life fhould be publifhed, which might confute the falfe reports already fpread abroad; and at the fame time fatisfy the defire which the faithful univerfally entertain of having a proper account of every thing relating to this Servant of God. This charge was confequently committed to me, becaufe I having been his Confeffor, it was imagined I might have a better knowledge of him than any other perfon. And as I was in duty bound, fo I readily confented to undertake it : to which I was alfo prompted by the efteem and affection which I always entertained for this poor Servant of Jefus Chrift, whofe life I now publifh.

The title prefixed to this work is fufficient to fhew, that my defign is to give fuch a clear account of this Servant of God, as may enable my read-

ers

ers to form a fufficient, if not a compleat idea of him: in confequence of which I have not fpared either labour, diligence, or endeavours to obtain the moft accurate intelligence concerning him. So that where I relate any facts that happened at a diftance from Rome, I have endeavoured by letters, and the help of friends, to procure the moft certain vouchers, as the reader will obferve in the courfe of the work: though I have often, for very good reafons, fuppreffed the names of the perfons from whom, and by whofe means, I obtained the faid intelligence.

I have alfo had in my poffeffion the authentick documents which have been tranfmitted to Rome by the Bifhop of Boulogne, which he ordered to be collected with the utmoft exactnefs, in the country where this Servant of God was born, and where he refided for feveral years: amongft which are the depofitions of his Father and Mother.

As to thofe things that have happened in Rome, I have heard the

accounts

accounts of them from perfons of the
utmoft veracity, who were eye-witneffes of the facts. Nor have I contented myfelf with having afked them
only on one occafion: but I have
often and at diftant periods of time,
interrogated them concerning the
things they related; on purpofe to fee
whether the accounts they gave afterwards, agreed with what they had faid
before. And I have moreover defired them to give me in writing under
their own hands, the accounts which
they had before given me by word of
mouth.

Neither have I relied on the teftimony of any perfon who did not declare himfelf ready to confirm his af-
fertion on oath in the Procefs of the
Beatification and Canonization of the
Servant of God, which is now going
on. For which reafon I have at proper times inferted the very words in
which the atteftations of the witneffes
are couched; which atteftations I now
have by me: and likewife a copy of
the Verbal Procefs, formed after his
death and before his burial. So that

I fhall

I shall not relate any thing but for which I can produce good vouchers.

I must also acquaint the benevolent reader, that in the many things concerning which I have not had recourse to any other person as a witness: it is, because I myself am voucher for them: as I, though unworthy, had the happiness to be his Director: and on that account have had many conversations with him, in which he has given me a most minute account of all the transactions of his life, even from his most tender years. Though, not to tire the reader, I shall not ordinarily in the course of this Life, mention those conversations: but only now and then, when I shall think it more necessary to manifest some glorious thing which happened to him, and which now appears to be verified. But although I have used all possible diligence and endeavours to acquire a true and perfect knowledge of what I relate; yet I may in some things be mistaken, as every man is liable so to be in human affairs. For which reason I desire no other credit than that of a Historian,

and

and such as may be due to the things which I relate. I hope the reader will excuse the stile being plain and common, such as is used by the common people: as what I write is designed to promote the good of all, by proposing to every reader, whether learned or unlearned, the virtuous examples of this Servant of God for his imitation: for which reason I have chose to relate his virtues, rather than his miracles. And where I have spoke of these, I have done it rather in general words, than given any particular account of them: as I thought it my duty so to do.

Lastly, In confirmation of what I have said at the beginning of this Preface, I think it proper here to mention the words of that worthy Priest Mr. Vincent, Rector of Oeuf a S. Pol, who expresses himself in his letter in the following manner: *The life of this man, which, till this present time, did not appear to have any thing remarkable in it, and was in a manner totally disregarded; now appears full of interresting and important matter, variegated with*

an

an infinite multitude of *circumstances*,
~~proved by a great multitude of witnesses~~,
and edifying in every one of its parts.
And such indeed was the life which he
led in all his pilgrimages, and here in
Rome itself. Wherefore, dear Reader, I will conclude with what S. Bernard says of S. Malachias. *You have
in him something to wonder at, and something to imitate.* Habes in illo quid
mireris, habes quid imiteris. This is
what I earnestly desire for your good:
for the glory of God: and for the ex-
altation of this his Servant.

THE

THE
TRANSLATOR'S PREFACE.

SCARCE had the accounts of the wonders wrought by the Almighty, at the Tomb, and by the Intercesſion, of this his Servant, arrived in England, but every one was deſirous of hearing them : and wiſhed to have them committed to the Preſs. It was however judged more prudent to wait, till information concering the particulars of his extraordinary life could be obtained and reduced into the form of a regular hiſtory: which muſt undoubtedly be more ſatisfactory to the publick, than the publication of unconnected pieces. This has now been done by the Rev. Mr. Joſeph Marcóni, the Confeſſor of Benedict, who publiſhed his Life in Italian: and an

abridgement

abridgement of it has been made in French: from which this edition is tranflated.

After what Mr. Marconi has faid in his Preface, it is ufelefs for me to add any thing more, either concerning the life itfelf, or the care which has been taken to give a true hiftory of this extraordinary man.

This edition confifts, firft, of a hiftory of the Life of this venerable Servant of God, from his birth till his body was laid in the grave: and which is a faithful tranflation from the French Edition, as any one may evidently fee who is acquainted with both the languages. To which I have added an Appendix, wherein I have given an account of feveral of the extraordinary cures faid to have been wrought both at his Tomb, and in other places, in favour of thofe who invoked his Interceffion, and defired him to pray for the relief of their refpective infirmities: which I have taken, partly from the Appendix to the French Edition of his life: and partly from original letters fent from Rome, and other places.

I have

I have already seen in the Gazetteer and New Daily Advertiser for October 5, 1784, a pretended extract of a letter from an English Gentleman at Boulogne, dated Sept. 27, wherein the writer publishes the fictions of his own brain under the title of Benedict's miracles. I say the fictions of his own brain; because that which he calls by the name of *Miracle*, No. 1, is every word of it an absolute Forgery: as nothing like is mentioned either in the printed account of Benedict's life, or in any letter sent from Rome relating to him. That which he calls *Miracle*, No. 2, has indeed some foundation: but is, according to the common practice of the Ridiculers of Miracles, misrepresented. Indeed, I do not in the least wonder at this; because, as this real or pretended letter-writer is fully convinced, that no Miracles were ever wrought in his Church: he thinks, the only way to save the credit of his Religion, is, to ridicule those which God is pleased, even now to work in the Church of Rome.

Those

Thofe who ridicule Miracles may be divided into two different claffes. The firft confifts of thofe perfons, who being profeffed Deifts, and denying all Revealed Religion, ridicule the Miracles of Mofes, the Prophets, and of Jefus Chrift himfelf, as well as thofe of all fucceeding ages. The other confifts of thofe who indeed profefs themfelves Chriftians, and believe the Miracles which are recorded in the Holy Scriptures, but at the fame time fay that Miracles have long ago ceafed in the Chriftian Church.

To thofe of the firft Clafs I fhall now fay nothing, as it is not at prefent my bufinefs to propofe the motives of Credibility for the converfion of Profeffed Infidels. But I think thofe of the fecond Clafs fhould not deny and ridicule Miracles, merely becaufe no Miracles were wrought in their own Church: left they fhould hereafter be found to be (as in reality they are) in circumftances exactly fimilar to thofe of the Scribes and Pharifees, who, fhut their eyes againft *the light that came*

to

to enlighten them that sat in darkness, and to guide their feet in the way of peace, and denied and resisted the miracles of Jesus Christ, which he wrought while he was on earth, to convince mankind that he was the promised Messias, and which *if he had not wrought, they would not have sinned in rejecting him:* but which being wrought, *they had no excuse for their sin.*

What is particularly remarkable in those Gentlemen, who ridicule the Miracles which God has in all ages continued to work, by the relicks and intercession of those who have served him faithfully on earth, and are now glorified by him in heaven; is, that they tread in the very steps of the Pharisees who rejected Christ, and his doctrine and miracles. When the man who was born blind had received his sight by the miraculous power of our Saviour, the Pharisees asked him how he had obtained his sight? * *He answered: That man that is called Jesus, made*

* John ix.

made clay, and anointed my eyes, and said to me: go to the pool of Siloe, and wash. And I went, I washed, and I see. They then would not believe that he ever had been blind: and examined his Parents, whether he was their son, and whether he was born blind? Concerning which when his parents had satisfied them: they still would not acknowledge the miracle. And when on another occasion * one was brought unto him, possessed with a devil, blind, and dumb; and he healed him, so that he both spoke and saw. Although this miracle was wrought in the presence of the Pharisees themselves, yet they would not acknowledge the power to be from God; but said: This man casteth out devils through Beelzebub the prince of the devils. In like manner, though miracles be wrought, though they be attested in the most authentick manner: yet those modern Pharisees, either deny the facts, attribute the accounts given of them to be some under-hand juggling, or which is more common

* Matth. xii. 22.

mon, endeavour to get rid of those stubborn proofs of the True Religion, by ridicule, when solid arguments fail them.

But, say they, we have very good reason to reject and look upon as impostures, all miracles said to be wrought in the Church of Rome; because all such miracles would tend to prove, a false, a superstitious, and idolatrous Religion to be the true pure Religion of Jesus Christ. This very thing shews still more how closely these Gentlemen tread in the steps of the Pharisees: and the argument which these make use of, is the very same which induced those to reject the miracles of Jesus Christ. They looked upon him to be an impostor, who had set himself up for the promised Messiah: an enemy to their Law; and the founder of a new Religion contrary to the Law of Moses: they had determined to put out of the Synagogue every one who believed in him: they looked upon all the miracles that he wrought, as tending to confirm that new, and as they thought, that false

Religion

Religion which he preached and pro-
pagated: they likewise accused him
of blasphemy, and took up stones to
throw at him for asserting that he was
the Messiah, and that he had existed
before Abraham; and moreover declared that he could not be a Prophet,
or from God, because he wrought
some of his miracles on the sabbath,
which they considered as a profanation
of that day. And in a word, the
Jewish Pharisees were as fully persuaded that no real miracle could be
wrought in confirmation of the Christian Religion which Jesus Christ then
preached: as our modern Christian
Pharisees are, that no real miracle can
be wrought in confirmation of the Religion taught in the Church of Rome.
As therefore, on the one hand, the miracles of Christ proved him to be the
promised one, and his doctrine divine:
so on the other, that doctrine, which is
confirmed by miracles wrought in the
name of Christ, must be the doctrine
he taught, and is thereby fully vindi-
cated from every aspersion of falsehood
or superstition.

It

It is the misfortune of the Chriſtian
Phariſees, as well as it was of the
Jewiſh Phariſees, to begin to examine
theſe ſubjects at the wrong end. That
is, they firſt lay it down as an undoubted principle, that the Church of
Rome is a ſuperſtitious and idolatrous
Church : and from thence they draw
this concluſion : That whatever miracles are ſaid to be wrought in the
Church of Rome, cannot be true miracles, but muſt neceſſarily be either
forgeries or juggles. That is, they
make the Doctrines the Teſt whereby
to judge of the truth of the miracles :
inſtead of making miracles the Teſt
whereby to judge of the Truth of the
Doctrines. Though if they would but
reflect on what they read in their
Bible, they would find that the power
of working miracles was given to Mo-
ſes, to the Prophets, and to the Apo-
ſtles, in order to convince mankind of
the Truth of their Doctrine, and that
they were commiſſioned by God to
teach it. And our Saviour himſelf
appealed to his miracles for the truth
of his doctrine, and of his being the

promiſed

promised Messias. For, says he, *if I had not done amongst them the works which no man ever did, they would not have had sin: but now they have no excuse for their sin.*

But, say they, Antichrist will work a great many lying signs and wonders, *insomuch as to deceive, if it were possible, even the very Elect.* And how then shall we know which are true, and which are false miracles; but only by the doctrines taught by those who perform those miracles? The words of our Saviour are very true: And the consequence they draw from them is also very true in the proper and peculiar sense and signification of the words of our Saviour: though not according to that extent to which Protestants want to strain them. Antichrist spoken of by our Saviour, as we learn from S. Paul, is that Man of Sin who will deny Christ, and set himself up in the Temple of God to be worshipped as God, and will do his endeavours to destroy the very name, as well as the publick profession of Christianity. And being assisted by infernal power, will

do

do many lying figns and wonders, whereby many will be deceived. But the Elect will avoid that deception, becaufe they will know and be firmly convinced, that according to the promifes of God in the Old Teftament, and of Jefus Chrift in the New, the Church which he eftablifhed is to laft for ever even to the end of the world. That it is not to be fucceeded by any other Religion, as was the cafe of the Law of Mofes. They will moreover remember, that Chrift has warned them of the coming of this man of perdition, and of the lying figns and wonders which he will work. And therefore they will conclude, that he who by his proceedings fulfils the prediction of Chrift and his Apoftles, by his denying Chrift, by endeavouring to deftroy the Religion of Chrift, and by fetting himfelf up in the temple of God, to be worfhipped as God; is that very man of perdition againft whom he has warned them. But as this man of perdition is only one fingle perfon, and as his proceedings will be fo dia-

metrically

metrically contrary to the Person and Religion established by Christ, that they who believe Christ to be *God blessed for ever*, cannot avoid knowing Antichrist by these signs : so this is the singular, the only case in which doctrines, once established by miracles, are to be the Test whereby Christians are to judge of the signs and wonders of Antichrist.

Moreover we know not of what kind, the lying signs and wonders which will be wrought by Antichrist will be : but this we know, that they will be *lying signs and wonders* : not real miracles, like those of Moses, the Prophets, of Christ, and the Apostles. But whenever any such miracles as were wrought by Christ and his Apostles, are or shall be *wrought by one who believes in Christ, and openly professes his Faith:* such miracles are always the work of God, done *by the finger of God:* and are always infallible vouchers of the truth of that Religion which he teaches or professes.

Those

Those who profess themselves Christians, and yet deny and ridicule all the miracles which have been properly vouched and attested, thoroughly examined, and solemnly approved as true miracles by the Church of God: would do well to confider what a handle they give to Deifts, and other profeffed Infidels, to deny all revealed religion, and to ridicule as impoftures, thofe miracles which are recorded in the very Scriptures themfelves. For all the books of the New Teftament, and confequently all the miracles therein recorded are handed down to us only by the teftimony of the fame Church of God. And confequently, all the certainty we can have that they are books written by the Apoftles, and by divine Infpiration, depends upon the veracity of the fame Church of God. And every Deift and other Infidel will very reafonably argue, that if the miracles faid to be wrought fince the days of the Apoftles are falfe and fictious, no one can fhew any reafon why thofe mentioned in the Scripture

should

should not be looked on in the same
light: for if it may be suppofed, that
the Church has forged the accounts of
thofe later miracles faid to have been
wrought fince the days of the Apoftles:
it may with equal propriety be suppofed, that fhe has forged the accounts
of the miracles faid to have been
wrought by Chrift and his Apoftles:
and likewife every thing elfe contained
in the books which relate them.

I will only add, that as Proteftants
generally pretend, that the Miracles
wrought in the Church of Rome are
*only wrought among themfelves, when
they are not needed, and where a free
enquiry into them is not allowed;* they
have now an opportunity, of making,
by the means of their Proteftant Cor-
refpondents refiding in Rome, all the
enquiries which their curiofity, or
their incredulity can fuggeft. But if
they think that enquiries by letters are
                                    too

* Dodwell's Free Anfwer to Middleton's Free
Enquiry into the Miraculous Powers of the
Primitive Church. p. 45.

too troublesome or too tedious, and have no objection against taking a short summer's jaunt for their diversion, to Amette, or Hesdigneul near Bethune in French Flanders: they will find hundreds of witnesses to attest so much concerning the former infirm state of Mary Helena Bayard, and her present healthy state; as likewise several witnesses (and among the rest the said Mary Helena Bayard herself) to attest the mode of cure: as will fully satisfy them that her cure was really miraculous. But if they now refuse or neglect to make this Enquiry: let them not pretend hereafter, that they have never had an opportunity of enquiring into the truth and reality of such Miracles.

THE

THE
LIFE

OF THE

SERVANT OF GOD.

BENEDICT JOSEPH LABRE.

CHAP. I.

*The Birth of the Servant of God; his Infancy
and Education.*

FRANCE, which is already so famous
in the Annals of Religion for the great
and holy men which it has produced, may
now exult on the increase of its glory, by
having produced in our age an extraordinary man, who during the whole course of
his life, being concealed among the common people, under the contemptible veil
of a poor, mean, and abject life; in the
very instant of his death, bursts from obscurity; and both by the sudden lustre of a
multitude of wonders which fame has pub-

lished

lifhed through all countries, and by the reputation of an eminent holinefs; fixes upon his Tomb the admiration of Rome, and the refpectful attention of the whole Catholick world.

By thefe faithful lineaments the Reader will immediately know that I allude to the Poor Servant of Jefus Chrift, Benedict Jofeph Labre, the relation of whofe life, according as the particulars of it may become publick, ought to form a tender and lafting impreffion of Religion and Piety in the heart of every Chriftian.

The Diocefs of Boulogne upon the Sea, was the happy country which gave birth to this Illuftrious Penitent. He was born in the Parifh of S. Sulpice of Ametta, on the 26th of March 1748, in the Pontificate of Benedict XIV. of immortal Memory, and in the glorious reign of Louis XV. of France.

His Father John Baptift Labre, and his Mother Anna Barbara Grandfire, are both yet living, in decent circumftances. God gave his bleffing to their marriage, and fent them fifteen children, of whom Benedict Jofeph was the eldeft. Their Patrimoney and their Bufinefs afforded them fufficient means to give a proper education and eftablifhment to their numerous family.

Touched with a proper fenfe of gratitude to God for the bleffings he had beftowed

ſtowed upon them, they diligently applied themſelves to train up their children in innocence and holineſs, and to ſet them an example of a meek and complaiſant behaviour, which ſtill continues to diſtinguiſh them among perſons of their own rank, and condition.

This Servant of God was Baptized by his Father's Brother, Mr. Francis Joſeph Labre, formerly Vicar, and afterward Rector of the Pariſh of Erin, in the Dioceſs of Boulogne, who was alſo his Godfather, and gave him the name of Benedict Joſeph. His Godmother was Anna Theodora Hazembergue.

Benedict Joſeph had the happineſs to have this Reverend Eccleſiaſtick for his Maſter, who took upon himſelf the care of his Education, and under whoſe inſtructions he paſſed the greateſt part of his youth.

He was formed to piety in his infancy, by the inſtructions and examples of his virtuous parents, who immediately endeavoured to unfold the precious buds which grace had ſhot forth in his Soul, and which ſpeedily produced the fruits of an innocent and holy life.

The Servant of God well knew the worth and importance of this firſt Education; he expreſſed his ſatisfaction and his gratitude for it, in a letter which he wrote to his Parents from Montreuil on the 2d

of

of October 1769, and he respectfully entreats them to educate his Brothers and Sisters according to the same plan. "This, "says he, is the means of making them "happy in Heaven: for without instruc-"tion they cannot be saved. I assure you "that you have now done with me: I "have cost you a great deal, but be assured "that, by the help of God's grace, I shall "reap the benefit of all that you have "done for me."

A solid judgment, a retentive memory, a quick apprehension even to liveliness, but to a liveliness tempered with a great deal of sweetness and docility; composed the Character of Benedict Joseph.

In him the first dawnings of reason appeared to be intermixed and confounded with the first rays of divine grace. His Soul immediately opened to, and entertained a tender devotion, which turned his first thoughts towards God. The Holy Ghost to render him more attentive to his inspirations, gave him, even from that time, a singular love of Prayer and Retirement. His Parents in their depositions, say that * they always remarked in him a disregard and contempt of childish amusements.

The

* Letter of M. Clement, Cannon, and Secretary to the Bishop of Boulogne, dated May 24. 1783.

The Holy Scripture gives this remarkable eulogium of young Tobias *, that though he was the youngeft of all thofe who compofed the Tribe of Nepthali, yet he did no childifh actions. And S. Bernard fpeaking of S. Malachias, gives an account of the firft years of his life, in the following words †. " His youth feemed " intended to render more amiable, and " attracting the holy gravity of old " men, whom he imitated in his conduct. " By his ferious and peaceable difpofition, " his fweet and ready obedience to his " fuperiors, his love of ftudy and of the " exercifes of young men; it feemed as if " the grace of God had utterly extinguifh- " ed in him all inclination to play and to " the amufements of children. And every " one admired in this child of benediction, " all the qualities and virtues of men who " had attained to years of perfect matu- " rity." And every one who gave teftimoney of what paffed in the infancy of Benedict Jofeph, applied to him the fame eulogium.

From the time he was five years of age, he fhewed a very earneft defire of learning

B 3   to

---

* Tobias, 1, 4.

† *Agebat fenem moribus, annis puer; expers lacivia puerilis, quietus et fubditus manfuetudini, non impatiens magifterii, non ludorum appetens.* S. Bern, in vita S. Malachiæ.

to read and write. This eagerness arose
from a holy impatience which he experienced of becoming better acquainted with
the Rudiments of Religion, by acquiring
a facility of reading them, and of writing
them with his own hand. A sensible joy
appeared in his countenance, when having learned to spell, he was able to read dif-
tinctly the words of the Lord's Prayer,
the Angelical Salutation, and the Apostles
Creed.

The operations of Grace, ought by no
means to be confounded with what is
purely the gift of Nature. The modera-
tion, the tranquility, and the sweet and
pacifick disposition, which constituted the
principal part of the character of Benedict
Joseph, and which appeared in him from
his earliest infancy were the works of
Grace, not the effect of constitution.

The particulars of his life furnish a great
number of proofs, that he was naturally
of a lively disposition: but a profound
humility which made him earnestly desire
to be disregarded, and even despised by
men, cast an impenetrable veil over, and
concealed from the eyes of mankind, these
natural qualities of his heart and of his
mind.

Being a descendant of Adam, he soon
perceived that there was in man a law in
the flesh, waging war against the law of his
mind. And being always obedient to the

motions

motions of Divine Grace, every affault of his paffions convinced him that the life of a chriftian in this world, is a continual warfare: and that a Soldier of Jefus Chrift muft never lay down his Arms, till the moment in which he is to receive his crown. From hence proceeded that courageous refolution, which he formed from his infancy, and which he firmly adhered to, of reftraining the firft motions of his natural paffions and inclinations, and of always correfponding with the grace of God, that in all things he might be guided entirely by the lights and motions of his Divine Spirit.

His Mafters, his Parents and other perfons, who had the care of him from his infancy, bear witnefs that they always obferved him to be naturally (as they thought) of a mild, and even bafhful temper. And thofe who have endeavoured to ftudy and penetrate into the fentiments and real motives of his conduct, look upon this teftimony as proofs that in him Grace triumphed over Nature. So that the humility which rendered him mean and contemptible in his own eyes; made him endeavour under the external appearance of fimplicity, to conceal the violence of his interior conflicts, and the merit of his victories over his natural difpofitions.

CHAP.

CHAP. II.

The same subject continued: the employments of the Servant of God in his Infancy.

THE infancy of those whom God has specially chosen to execute the extraordinary decrees of his Divine Providence, is almost always a kind of miniature of what they will be, when arrived at years of maturity. And we are furnished with a new proof of this truth in the life of Benedict.

Corresponding with the motions of Divine Grace, which indicated to what kind of life he was called by God, he at five years of age began to execute the resolution of making his Soul as much as possible, a most perfect model and copy of our Divine Saviour Jesus Christ.

This was one of his common and frequent reflections, that a Christian who sincerely desires perfectly to imitate and become conformable to Jesus Christ, ought to have in some manner three hearts, founded on, proceeding from, and concentered in one: that is to say. One for God, another for his neighbour; and the third for himself.

The first, said he, ought to be pure and sincere, always tending to an eminent degree of holiness: continually aspiring

to

to the love of God, with a defire to ferve him, and to fubmit with patience and refignation to every affliction with which it fhall pleafe him to afflict us during the courfe of this mortal life.

The fecond heart, faid he, ought to be faithful, generous, and inflamed with charity for our neighbour, always ready to ferve him, and particularly employed in fighs and prayers, for the converfion of finners, and for the relief of the faithful departed.

The third, faid he, ought to be fteady in its firft refolutions, auftere, mortified, zealous and courageous, continually offering itfelf in facrifice to God. Such ought to be the heart of a Chriftian, who being the difciple of a crucified God, will not allow of any gratification of his fenfual inclinations, but keeps his body in fubjection by the wholefome feverities of felf-denial; and is perfuaded that the happinefs of the next life will be proportioned, to the contempt, which in this life he has entertained for this finful body to which he is chained; and the courage and refolution with which he has kept it nailed to the Crofs.

In fine, faid he, thefe three hearts, or affections ought to be fo united as to make only one, which fhould be amiable to all, a friend of peace, and above all truly humble: for whofoever builds upon any other foundation than that of humility,

builds

builds upon fand. Such were the great ideas, which from the moft tender age this child of Grace entertained concerning the perfection of a Chriftian life.

In order to form within himfelf by the help of divine grace, this firft Heart, which ought to be dedicated entirely to divine love: he took for the rule of his conduct, a purity of confcience eafily to be alarmed and terrified even with the flighteft faults: fuch a horror of fin as made him dread and avoid the lighteft occafions of temptation, an exact correfpondence with every divine infpiration, and a lively and active faith continually attentive to, and fixed on his divine pattern.

Conformable to his idea of forming a heart inflamed with Charity for his neighbour, he made a refolution of always expreffing the real fentiments of his foul, with fimplicity, franknefs, and candour; of excluding from his thoughts all rafh judgments and fufpicions; of loving his neghbours with a difinterefted love; and of offering himfelf to ferve them by every means which his zeal could fuggeft: but above all, to affift them by his prayers, which was the means moft in his power, and which at the fame time appeared to him to be the beft and moft efficacious.

And to form in himfelf a heart which might be conformable to that of his crucified Saviour, he refolved to make it his in-
                                                    difpenfable

dispensable practice, to *chastise his body and
bring it into subjection*, by a privation of all
sensual satisfactions, by the exercise of continual self-denials and mortifications, and
by treating it with a great deal of contempt;
that thereby he might prevent any rebellion of the flesh against the law of the
Spirit.

Nothing can be more edifying than these
maxims which he laid down as the foundation of an Evangelical life; and to which
he perceived in himself a particular vocation.

His first maxim was to entertain an
equal degree of distrust in his own strength,
and of confidence in the succours of the
grace of God: the second was to apply
himself without ceasing to acquire a true
knowledge of God, and of himself: the
third was, to die to himself, that he might
live only, and according to, the life of his
crucified Saviour: and the fourth, courageously to put on the armour of God,
which is, prayer, mortification, a renunciation of the world and its dangerous allurements; and above all interiour solitude,
and a life of prayer, which is the school of
true wisdom, and has always been fruitful
in producing holy and evangelical souls.

To declare what were his maxims and
his resolutions is just the same thing as to
say, what was the continual practice of his
life. The testimony given by his parents
proves how exactly he observed these max-

ims

ims even from his moft tender years *: " In " proportion, fay they, as he advanced in " age, he increafed alfo in wifdom both " before God and man."

In his infancy, inftead of other childifh plays he ufed to make little Oratories, which was a prefage of that devotion, which during the whole courfe of his life inclined him to look upon as a particular favour the being permitted to ferve the Prieft at the Celebration of the Sacred Myfteries. A practice for which, as his parents teftify, he always had a great defire.

A refpect for the Churches was another of the virtues which was particularly remarkable in his infancy. Being ftruck with the Majefty of thofe facred places, and with the fanctity of the venerable Myfteries therein celebrated, he never entered into them, but with fuch a degree of reverence as afforded edification to every beholder.

When a Soul is free from every earthly affection, and full of God, whom the livelinefs of it's faith reprefents as being in a ftate of immolation upon the altars ; when a Soul is truly fenfible of, and truly grateful for all his favours; where can fuch a Soul experience more celeftial fweetnefs than in the Temples and before the holy Altars? After the firft fketches which we

have

* Depofition of his Father and Mother.

have given of the infancy of Benedict, we ought not to be furprized at what we learn from a multitude of winesses, as well with regard to his readinefs and diligence in affifting at the Divine Service, as with regard to the tender devotion and holy eagernefs with which he fought after inftruction in the principles of Chriftianity. The principal occupations, and almoft the only delights of this Servant of God in his tender age, were to hear, to read, and meditate on the word of God.

In France, and principally in the country places, on Sundays and feftival days, after having affifted at the Evening Office of the Church, it is the cuftom of the people to fpend the reft of the day in different recreations. The complaifance and refpect which Benedict entertained for the will of his Parents and his Mafters feem to have been the only motives which led him to thefe publick amufements: * " but with-
" out any relifh or inclination for thefe
" diverfions; on the contrary, he would
" frequently leave them to go and con-
" verfe with more aged and ferious per-
" fons."

There are a great number of children whofe giddinefs and levity is unconquerable; they fatigue themfelves by their natural vivacity, and every day form new

C   inclinations

* Depofition of his Father and Mother.

inclinations and with the utmost eagerness pursue every object of pleasure which presents itself to their imagination. There are also some others whose indifference for pleasures proceeds from nothing but a mere stupidity of Soul, and whose apparent early gravity, is nothing but the effect of a melancholick disposition. But the gravity and recollection of young Labre, and his retiring from the ordinary amusements of those of his age, proceeded from a pure and exalted motive. For whensoever either obedience or civility rendered it a kind of duty, he would always with a good grace engage in innocent diversions. He was, says his Uncle M. Vincent, " always chearful in his recreations, and " contented with his companions."

If then while he was an infant we find in him none of the defects of infants, if we find in him nothing of that giddiness, levity, impatient desires, no disgust against spiritual things, no repugnance to labour, no love of that liberty and independence which we generally remark in other children: this can be attributed only to God who was pleased to enlighten his budding reason, and incline him to contemn the ordinary imperfections and follies of that age: and to instruct his young Soul in the knowledge of the means that were most proper to curb his natural vivacity, and restrain the first sallies of self-love. This can

be

be attributed only to the grace of Jesus Christ, who designed to make him a model of the most profound humility; in good time gave him to understand, and seriously to reflect on that word which he always addresses to those whom he calls to a state of perfection. "*Learn of me, for I am* "*meek and humble of heart.*"

The young Labre at the same time began to shew an early desire and relish of silence and retirement. For the Holy Ghost, who was pleased to choose from a class of men whom our pride and vanity looks on with disdain, a striking model of devout and contemplative life: from that time engaged Benedict to follow his vocation, and taught him by a happy experience, in what manner the pleasures which the communication with mankind affords, leave an emptiness in the Soul, which has begun to be united to its God by silence and retirement.

Nevertheless this serious and composed disposition of the Servant of God, did not hinder any one from remarking in him, and even in his countenance, signs of a free and open disposition, and a fund of chearfulness which was natural to him, which he preserved all his life, and the influence of which every one perceived who looked upon him with attention.

The age of infancy terminated much sooner in him than in the generality of

children.

ple left in his foul. " I always knew him
" fays he in one of his letters, to be a child
" of an admirable good difpofition, and of
" a fingular and exemplary diligence in
" difcharging the duties corresponding to
" his age, and endowed with every good
" quality which I could wifh to find in a
" child; and which rendered his memory
" fo dear to me, that for the fpace of about
" eight and twenty years fince he left me
" I never let flip any opportunity of en-
" quiring after him; fo much did I expect
" that fome good would attend him."

To this is added the declaration of Francis Jofeph Forgeois, who fays; * " That he
" remarked in this child, that he diftin-
" guifhed himfelf from all the others of his
" age, by his modefty, his piety, his doci-
" lity, his meeknefs, his tranquility, and
" his eagernefs to learn to read, and to
" learn the firft Principles of Religion."——
And Bartholomew Francis de la Rue, another of his mafters declares, that " he re-
" marked in him a great deal of piety, do-
" cility, meeknefs, and complaifance for
" his mafter; that he never had occafion
" to be affraid of his mafter; as being fen-
" fible of his having never given him oc-
" cafion of offence. He moreover de-
" clares that he himfelf was fo well fatisfied
" with

* Francis Jofeph Forgeois was a Servant of
M. D'Hanotel.

" with the conduct of Benedict, that he
" does not remember, he ever said or did
" any thing that might grieve him."

God has been pleased that the education
of Benedict in the first years of his life,
should be commited to several masters suc-
cessively in order that by that means he
might multiply witnesses of the virtues and
extraordinary graces with which he was favoured in his infancy. He in a particular
manner possessed all the virtues suitable to
that age: a scrupulous diligence in the dis-
charge of his duties, love of study, respect
for his parents, docility and obedience to
his masters and civility to all. But what
appeared to be far beyond the capacity of a
child, and which neverthelefs was the singular character of Benedict, was even at
that time a sensible love of retirement and
recollection, a remarkable disengagement
of his heart from all affection to earthly
things, a reigning inclination for piety: and
to say all in one word, an anticipated knowledge of that true Christianity which does
every thing for the love of God, which
tends continually towards God, and which
in all things endeavours to imitate the poverty and humility of its crucified Saviour.

Let us not by any means pretend to
measure the wisdom of God by the dimi-
nutive scale of the human understanding.
God is wonderful in all his Saints. His
Providence

Providence shines upon his Church in
every age with great lustre, and in such a
manner as renders it more and more vi-
sible. In all probability the reason why
God imparted to Benedict while he was
yet an infant, such extraordinary graces;
was, that by new examples capable of
arousing our drowsy faith; he might convince us, that his Church, which is always
Holy, will never cease to have Saints of
every age, as well as it has Saints in every
state and condition of life.

CHAP. IV.

*An Account of the Youth of Benedict. His
Conduct under the Direction of his Uncle:
He makes his first Communion.*

ST. BERNARD by these remarkable
words describes the transition of St.
Malachias, from a state of infancy to that
of youth.
  * " The youth of St. Malachias, was en-
" tirely of a piece with his infancy. He
" preserved the same purity, the same sim-
" plicity, the same innocence of morals.
" The only difference that could be ob-
               " served

* *Et ejus quidem pueritia sic erat. Porro adole-
scentiam simili transivit simplicitate & puritate;
nisi quod crescente ætate, crescebat simul ille sapien=*

" ferved in him in thofe two different
" ftages of his life was, that in his youth
" he entertained a ftill greater defire to
" grow in wifdom and in grace both with
" God and man: in fuch manner that be-
" fides the common obligations incumbent
" on him, he took upon himfelf certain
" particular devotions and obfervances;
" and by this means raifed himfelf to a de-
" gree of virtue and holinefs to which it
" was difficult for others to attain."

We may obferve a ftriking likenefs between this eulogium which St. Bernard
gives of the adolefcence of St. Malachias,
and the expreffions which the Parents of
Benedict made ufe of in giving an account
of the conduct of their Son, from his infancy till he was about twelve years old, which
was the time when he left his Father's
houfe, and was put under the care of his
Uncle the Reverend Rector of Erin.

We may fee in this happy refemblance
between thefe two Characters, and with a
fatisfaction which is well able to animate
our Faith, that it is always the fame Divine
Spirit who makes Saints: and that though
the fruits of his graces may be different,
according to the difference of the ages and
ftates

tia & gratia apud Deum & homines. Nifi quod
præter inftituta communia, multa fingulariter facie-
bat, in quibus potius præibat omnes, & aliorum
nemo poterat ad tam ardua jequi. S. Bern. iu
vita S. Malachiæ.

ſtates of the perſons to whom he imparts them; yet that the ſource, the foundation, and the ſubſtance of the ſanctity from whence theſe fruits proceed, is the ſame in every age, and in every ſtate: and that by a particular diſpoſition of his Divine Providence, it ſometimes happens that children called in their infancy and at the firſt hour to a life of holineſs, and who perſevere faithful to their vocation, may be propoſed as models to thoſe perſons who ſeem not to hear till the laſt hours of their life that voice of God which never ceaſes to call them to a life of holineſs.

This concluſion naturally follows from the idea formed in our minds, by the multitude of teſtimonies of the conduct of Benedict in the courſe of his infancy and of his youth. " His parents in particular de-
" clare, that during the time he continued
" under their care, he gave them conſtant
" proofs of a ſincere piety; by his aſſiſting
" at the Divine Offices and inſtructions
" with a degree of attention and reverence
" truly edifying; of wiſdom and prudence,
" in never ſaying or doing any thing un-
" becoming: of obedience, by always do-
" ing what he was ordered, with chearful-
" neſs and alacrity: of Peacefulneſs, in al-
" ways behaving towards his father, his
" mother, his brothers, and ſiſters in ſuch
" manner, as never to give them any oc-
" caſion of uneaſineſs or offence: and of a
" wonderful

" wonderful patience, by bearing the weak-
" neſſes and imperfections of his father,
" his mother, his brothers, his ſiſters, and
" thoſe of his age; always maintaining a
" ſerene and chearful countenance not-
" withſtanding whatever they ſaid or did
" to him; and this to ſuch a degree, as to
" make thoſe who had been culpable, a-
" ſhamed of their proceedings.—A diſpo-
" ſition (add his parents) which rendered
" this child moſt dear and amiable to them,
" as he likewiſe was to every one who
" knew him."

The Parents of young Labre being
charmed with the good qualities of his heart
and of his ſoul, thought that they ought to
concur with the deſigns of God concerning
him, by procuring for him, jointly with
the knowledge of the Latin Tongue, an
education ſuperior to that which he would
be able to obtain while he ſhould continue
in his Father's houſe.

M. Labre, who was both his Uncle and
his Godfather, received from the hands of
his parents this young plant, who had already afforded ſuch promiſing hopes to all
thoſe who had had him under their care,
and had given him, the firſt cultivation.
Benedict during his whole life looked upon
it as a ſingular favour of divine Providence,
that in the moſt critical age of youth he
had been committed to the care and affection of this worthy Eccleſiaſtick, in whom
he

he all at once found a Preceptor, a Spiritual Director, a Friend, and a Pattern for his Imitation.

The Servant of God being then in the twelfth year of his age: his virtuous uncle thought he ought to begin his course of education, by disposing him to make his first Communion: and therefore gave him notice to prepare himself for it.

At this news his Soul was filled with sentiments of joy: of love, of humility, and of a holy fear. These words of the Apostle, *Let a man prove himself, and so let him eat of that heavenly bread,* were the most common subject of his thoughts. He had for a long time sighed after this happiness, for which by a long practice of meditation he had acquired the greatest esteem. Before the approach of this happy day he used his utmost endeavours to cleanse and purify his soul by a General Confession. And this was the first out of five or six General Confessions which he made in the course of his life.

The method which he took to prepare himself for the Sacrament of Pennance, is so edifying, that it will without doubt be both agreeable and useful to give a particular account of it.

The venerable Benedict being persuaded that without the grace of God we can do nothing, no not even discover our own faults so as to view them in that light in which

which we ought to confider them, firft implore the light of the Holy Ghoft, and befought him not only to bring to his remembrance his fins with all their different circumftances; but likewife to difcover to him the true ftate of his foul, his biafs, and inclinations.

After this he ferioufly examined into the ftate of his confcience, proceeding according to the order of the Commandments, and to the virtues correfponding to each Commandment; therewith examining and comparing his life and all his actions, from the time he had made his laft Confeffion.

When he examined his confcience for a General Confeffion, he divided his life into fo many fpaces of time as he had made general confeffions after his firft Communion: and then began with the laft Epoch, and went back in regular order from that to the firft.

In the courfe of this examination he took fpecial care not to make himfelf the judge of his own actions; this he confidered as the province and privilege of the Minifter of Jefus Chrift. And therefore that he might not tranfgrefs his own bounds, he explained what temptations he had experienced, and how he had behaved under them: as likewife what fpecial graces he had received from Almighty God, and gave a particular account in what manner he had correfponded with them.

D

The

The examination of his confcience being finifhed, he again had recourfe to
humble and fervent prayer to obtain of
God a true contrition of heart, and endeavoured to excite this contrition in his foul,
by a ferious confideration of all the motives
which Faith fuggefts as leading to it.
Above all he endeavoured to excite in his
foul a forrow for fin founded on thofe motives which render it *perfect contrition*, by
confidering fin as an ingratitude committed
againft God, a difobedience to his law, and
an outrage offered to his infinite and effen-
tial fanctity. And in his accufation of himfelf he preferved order, clearnefs, precifion,
humility, and fincerity, to an admirable
degree.

After this he liftened to the words of his
Confeffor with very great refpect, fubmit-
ing his own private opinions to his deci-
fions, being docile to his inftructions, and
venerating his word as oracles fent from
heaven.

Before receiving the Abfolution he
bowed himfelf down; and, for fome time
humbling himfelf in the prefence of Almighty God, renewed his forrow for his
fins, and endeavoured to excite in his foul
moft lively acts of contrition: after which
he modeftly raifed his head to give his
Confeffor to underftand that he was now
ready to receive abfolution.

He

He was perfuaded in his own mind, and frequently repeated to others this idea, which he faid he learnt from S. Terefa, that a multitude of Chriftians plunge them-felves into eternal miferies by making fa-crilegious Confeffions. He diftinguifhed the finners who went to Confeffion, into three claffes: the perfect penitents, the im-perfect penitents, and the falfe penitents; who appeared to him, as forming three Proceffions of people, who in departing from the facred Tribunal of Penance, took each a different road.

The firft clafs, which confifted of but very few, was compofed of true penitents: thefe were they who having probed the wounds of their fouls to the bottom: had manifefted them with fincerity and without difguife; had entertained a fincere forrow for them; had bewailed them with truly penitential tears; and without having neg-lected any of the conditions neceffary for a good Confeffion, had afterwards ufed their utmoft efforts to appeafe the divine juftice, by their fafts, their prayers, their alms, and other mortifications, and exer-cifes of piety fuperadded to the penitential works enjoined them by the Minifters of God; and had endeavoured, by faithfully performing the conditions required for the gaining of Indulgences, to fupply what was ftill wanting in them to fulfill all juftice. The Servant of God looked upon thefe holy

penitents

penitents as being cloathed with a white
and luminous robe: who in the moment of
their death are carried to heaven, and enter
in triumph into the eternal Tabernacles of
the living God.

The second clafs, ftill very few, yet more
numerous than the former, was compofed
of imperfect penitents, who had their garments tinged of a red colour. Thefe were
they who had indeed faithfully complied
with the conditions effentially neceffary for
a good confeffion, and had not rendered
the grace of pennance ufelefs. But relying
too much on the pardon they had obtained, they had afterwards fhewn but very
little zeal in performing the penitential
works prefcribed them by their Confeffor:
and had neglected to have recourfe to the
Indulgences, which their tender and com-
paffionate mother the Church offers to its
penitent and reconciled children, to put
them in the way of fupplying their own infufficiency of fatisfying the divine juftice
for their fins. Heaven, faid he, remains
fhut againft their defires of entering: and
they are pufhed back towards purgatory to
compleat that fatisfaction, which the Divine Juftice demands, and to be entirely
purified from every thing which has defiled
their fouls.

The falfe Penitents who compofed the
third clafs, and which was far more numerous than the two former, appeared to
him

him as cloathed with dirty and filthy garments.: Thefe were they, who either by hafte and extraordinary negligence in the examination of their confcience, by being deftitute of true contrition or a firm refolution of amendment, by want of fincerity in the acknowledgement of their fins, or by being overcome by a wretched fear or fhame, wilfully concealed any part of their fins; and by that means defiled their fouls with the very waters of that facred bath which was intended to reftore them to their original purity : thefe appeared to him as facrilegious hypocrites, who go to hell by the very road which ought, and was intended to lead them to heaven.

These thoughts ftrongly imprinted in the mind of Benedict a dread and horror of fin. And they contributed to preferve and defend his innocence againft temptations, and to render beneficial to him the ufe of the Sacraments, to which he had recourfe to be purified from his fins.

A general confeffion made according to the method of Benedict, is undoubtedly an excellent preparation for the firft communion. To which preparation he alfo added Meditation, Prayer, and fome particular acts of Mortification.

We know fays St. Thomas * what effects the Bread which came down from

Heaven

* S. Thomas, Opufc. de Ven. Sacr. Alt.

Heaven produces, when it is received into a Soul well prepared for it. As it is the Bread of Angels it makes us pure like them: as it is the Blood of God, it in some manner transforms us into God: as it is the tree of life, planted in the hearts of the faithful, it fails not immediately to produce both the flowers which exhale the good odour of true disciples of Jesus Christ, and the plentiful fruits of every Christian virtue.

Those which the grace of his first Communion produced in this Servant of God, immediately manifested themselves by a sensible increase of his fervour and piety, and by a more close and perfect union with God: for from this moment he turned all his thoughts and affections towards Heaven: continually endeavouring to make his Soul a lively model of Jesus Christ, and continually aspiring to such a degree of perfection, that he might say with the Apostle, *I live, or rather it is not I, but Christ who liveth in me.* But his inclination to works of Penance and Mortification was still more sensible; for from that time, he began to observe all the fast days appointed by the Church with scrupulous exactness: and such was his temperance and niceness in this point, that he would rather tread under his feet the most delicious fruits of his Uncle's garden, than

offer

offer to tafte any of them, which were moft capable of alluring him.

He entertained a ftill more ardent love for his neighbour, for they now began to take notice that he abridged himfelf of his neceffary fuftenance, that he might fecretly convey to a poor woman, that food which was given to him for his own nourifhment, and, in this manner by one and the fame act practifed the two Chriftian virtues of Penance and Almfgiving.

He had alfo a ftill more evident love of folitude and retirement: for from this time he began to entertain a total difre-gard for the world, and all his thoughts and converfation turned towards Heaven *. " From this time his only delight was to " remain either at the foot of the Altars, " or in a little fummer houfe at a diftance " from his Uncle's dwelling houfe, and " where he was almoft continually occu- " pied in reading books of Piety."

CHAP.

* Depofition of Mr. Viroux.

CHAP. V.

Sentiments of Esteem which the Uncle, and the School-fellows of the Servant of God, entertained for him.

IT commonly happens that a virtuous man gains an ascendant, and a certain kind of natural authority over them with whom he lives, which procures him both their esteem and respect; and which almost always tends to promote piety and virtue among them.

After the description we have already given of the qualities and virtues of this Servant of God; we ought not to be astonished at any of those things that are reported of him, at the impression which his conduct made on the hearts of those who were eye-witnesses of his actions, or at the sentiments and marks of friendship, esteem, nd respect which they shewed him.

* " The children, says Mr. Emadon, " Rector of Erin, paid to him at least as " great respect, as they did to their Master on account of his Piety." This testimony agrees with that which is given by M. Clement, who says, " That the children observed something in him which " inspired them with more respect for
" him

* Letter of Mr. Emadon Rector of Erin.

" him, than the prefence of even their
" Mafter himfelf produced." This is
likewife attefted by many of his former
fchoolfellows, when they were feparately
interrogated, in what manner he ufed to
conduct himfelf in his youth; and whofe
depofitions are contained in the letter of
the Reverend Rector of Erin, He fays,
" They, (Jofeph Briffel, James le Gay,
" and James Louis Thuilliers,) have all
" declared, and affured me, that, they al-
" ways obferved him to be very prudent
" and exemplary in his conduct; that he
" feverely reprimanded them, when he
" faw them do, or heard them fpeak any
" thing improper, or contrary to the com-
" mandments of God: that he was very
" pious, modeft, and devout in the
" Church; that he conftantly affifted at
" all the divine offices, without ever
" moving himfelf; that he always applied
" himfelf diligently to read good books;
" that inftead of eating the food that was
" given to him, he would frequently give
" it to fome poor perfon out of the win-
" dow; that when he went to take a walk
" or other recreation with his Uncle the
" Rector, he carried with him fome books
" of piety, and read them as he walked
" along; and in a word that all the time
" he lived in the parifh of Erin, they
" never faw him do, or heard him fpeak
" any

" any thing, that was any way improper,
" or contrary to good manners."

Next to that sweetness which flows into
the Soul of a pious Christian by conversing
with God in Prayer, it can experience
none greater than that of hearing God
speak to it by the means of good books;
in which employment the Servant of God
employed every moment of time he could
find otherwise vacant. Among the books
belonging to his Uncle, he found the
Sermons of Pere le Jeune the Oratorian,
who is also and more commonly known by
the name of Pere l'Aveugle.

The force of his reasoning, founded entirely on the evidence of good sense, the
bewitching smoothness of his kind of florid
style, the simplicity, and if I may so call
it, the popularity of his expressions, would
naturally produce in a Soul an imagination disposed like that of Benedict, a certain kind of interested pleasure, flowing
from a conformity of sentiment; and
which in effect it did produce in him.
For which reason he made the Sermons
of this Preacher his favourite books: he
had them continually in his hands, and a
great and happy memory preserved during
his whole life, the deposited truths of
Christian Morality, which the frequent
reading of these Sermons had deeply imprinted in his Soul.

Fear

[35]

. Fear and love are the two springs which act most powerfully upon the human heart. And Pere le Jeune makes use of these with a great deal of force and pathetick sensibility, particularly in his two Sermons, on Hell, and on the small number of the Elect. These Sermons, made a very deep impression in the soul of this pious young man; and the more so, as he read them at a time when he began seriously to think on choosing a state of life, and this made him redouble his fervour in his prayers, and beg of God to direct him by his grace to choose that, to which his Divine Providence should be pleased to call him.

The pious young man was now near entering into the sixteenth year of his age. And a delicate and timorous conscience, a courageous heart, and a generous Soul, trained up from his infancy in the purest and most solid maxims of Piety and Religion, would naturally incline him to embrace a state, which might furnish his ardent spirit with the means which were most likely to raise him to the utmost pitch of human perfection. His inclination to solitude, his retirement and separation from the world, his love of Prayer, and of the exercises of Piety, which the frequent participation of the Holy Sacraments daily more and more augmented in him; immediately turned his thoughts

towards

greater referve in his conduct, greater fimplicity in his manners, greater feparation from worldly pleafures, and a greater defire of uniting his Soul more clofely to God by a frequent participation of the Holy Sacraments.

His Uncle's houfe was to him a kind of Monaftery; where, as much as his fituation would allow, he obferved a religious poverty, the filence of a cloifter, and all the regularity of a religious community. His fubmiffion and ready obedience to the will of his Uncle, was like that of a Religious man to his Superior. Being already accuftomed to the aufterities of a penitential life, he rigoroufly obferved all the Faft days commanded by the Church, although by his not having yet attained to twenty-one years of age, he was exempt from the Law of Fafting. Such was the conduct of this Servant of God for the fpace of two years and a half, which he fpent at Erin: whofe virtues are ftill frefh in the minds, highly efteemed, and frequently fpoken of by the inhabitants of that place; the greateft part of whom had been eye-witneffes of his conduct. And the proofs he afforded them of his charity for them, will for a long time render them grateful to his memory.

A cruel epidemick diforder defolated that Parifh; fo that every houfe was full of perfons attacked with it; infomuch, that there was fcarce any perfon who was

able

able to supply the wants of the sick, or to attend and serve them. These and such like misfortunes to which human nature is subject; almost always furnish Religion with matter of triumph; because they always afford a true Christian occasions of exercising his virtues; for he scarce knows how valuable his life is, but only at the time when he has an opportunity of making a sacrifice of it to God, by serving his brethren.

The virtuous Uncle on this occasion shewed his zeal and love for his Parishioners to be boundless: and the charity of this pious young man inspired him with courage and resolution to brave every danger. To neither Uncle nor Nephew did the night afford any rest, after the fatigue of the day: but each one, without any relaxation, went hither and thither to afford relief, wherever danger called them; so that there was no one sick person in the whole Parish, who was not visited, served, comforted, and assisted.

In country places, the cattle constitute a great part of the fortune of the poor Farmers; insomuch that to lose their cattle, is to them an evil almost as great as to lose their own lives. Benedict knew this, and therefore he endeavoured to render them all the service that was in his power by dividing his labours, partly in taking care of the poor sick persons: and partly in taking care of the cattle that belonged to them.

While

While his Uncle, wholly employed in the exercise of his Pastoral Office, exposed his life in visiting and comforting the sick, and stripped himself of all that he was worth, to afford relief to his poor Parishioners; this charitable young man performed for them the most abject and laborious services. He took care of their cattle, cleaned their stalls: and he, who by the life he had lived with his Uncle, and whose education seems to have forbid him to be employed in menial labours; might be frequently seen running sometimes to the gardens, sometimes to the fields, and returning again loaded with greens, grafs, and provender for the cattle and other animals, the care of which he had taken upon himself, and which he distributed to them with his own hands.

So great charity is never exercised without meeting with a proper reward. God who keeps an account of every cup of cold water given in alms for his sake, without doubt will never forget it: but how different are the thoughts of God, and how much more exalted, than the thoughts of man! The world sometimes gives wealth or titles of honour as the reward of past services; but God frequently sends to his friends new crosses to endure, as the recompense of what they have already done or suffered for his sake. And what is this but the fulfilling those words of our Saviour:

our: *Woe be to them who have received their consolation here*, by which our infinitely wise, and good God gives us to under-stand that he does not confound the time of combat, with the time of triumph, and of receiving the reward of our victories: but that the most precious recompence for past services which a Christian ought to desire, so long as he shall continue in this life, is that, of new occasions of serving, and fulfilling the will of God here, and thereby meriting a more glorious crown hereafter.

It was in this manner that God was plea-sed to deal with this his Servant. The Epi-demical disorder after a time ceased: but the excess of fatigue had totally exhausted the strength of the worthy Rector of Erin. A fit of sickness, which was the consequence of it, in a few days carried him out of this world, to the great grief of the inhabitants of the parish, who for a long time regreted the loss of their worthy Pastor.

What a stroke was this for Benedict, and in what a situation was he left! God had deprived him of a master, a patron, a second father. In his house he found a retreat, which in a great measure alleviated the regret he experienced at finding the Monasteries shut against him, by his parents refusing their consent. But the death of his Uncle left him almost without support, and seemed to be a presage of new obsta-

cles

cles to the following his vocation. The Servant of God faw the whole extent of his
lofs: neverthelefs his courage increafed
with his confidence in God: and the Holy
Ghoft fpeaking interiourly to his foul, gave
him to underftand that a Chriftian is never
ftronger, than when he has no reliance but
on God alone.

CHAP. VII.

He returns again to his Parents, and again
endeavours to obtain their confent for him
to go to La Trappe.

THE idea and reprefentation of his
Uncle in the agonies of death was
deeply and laftingly imprinted in the mind
of this Servant of God, and was in a manner continually before his eyes. It is in
this fchool of the contemplation of death
that true Chriftians are formed to virtue.
That important moment difcovers the true
value of Time and Eternity. For to a
wife man who feeks truth with fincerity of
heart, and who, upon the Tomb of a
perfon who was once dear to him, reads
with attention, the fragility of man's
life, and the vanity of the world; God
immediately becomes the only object of
his defires. Thefe kind of reflections
                                    contributed

contributed to awaken in Benedict the thoughts of retirement, and the desire of solitude, that he might have nothing to do but to labour for the salvation of his Soul. His humility inclined him to believe, that the true obstacle to the success of his hopes and endeavours, was his own unworthiness: and for this reason he used all possible means to render Almighty God propitious to him. He increased the number of his prayers, and redoubled his fervour in his devotions. And by the practice of works of penance and particular mortifications, he laid deep the foundation of that life of poverty, austerity, and self-denial, which he afterwards carried to so great a degree of perfection.

It was at this time that he made his second general Confession, in order to prepare himself to lead a life more holy, more united to God, and more worthy of being admitted into a Religious state, which was the constant object of his wishes.

The Servant of God being now again returned to his parents after the death of the venerable Rector of Erin, took this occasion to solicit their consent for him to enter into a Religious House: and that they would give him leave to go to the Abbey of La Trappe. But he now met with a second repulse, still stronger than that which he had experienced before: particularly from his mother, who was en-

couraged

couraged in her refusal, by the concurrent oppofition which the whole family made to his propofal.

But being now eighteen years old, he thought that he might fhew more firmnefs and refolution, without any ways deviating from the refpect due to his parents. He forcibly urged to them the neceffity of following his vocation: and fhewed them that the reafons which fhocked their tendernefs, and engaged them to endeavour to turn his thoughts from the refolution he had taken of choofing to go to La Trappe, ought on the contrary to encourage them: becaufe, faid he, a conftant inclination to a clofe retirement and to the exercifes of the holy aufterities of a penitential life, is the moft certain fign of a vocation to a Religious ftate.

The parents of Benedict having always been very religious: they apprehended that by longer refifting the defires of their Son, they might probably be found to have refifted what was the will of God. The Servant of God, in confequence of this idea, at length obtained their confent and their benediction. He accordingly left them: and the fatigue of a long journey did nothing but augment his zeal, and defires of living a poor and mortified life.

What a multitude of fentiments of joy prefented themfelves to the foul of the Servant of God as foon as he arrived within in fight of the Abbey of La Trappe! He now thought himſelf ſecure of the object of his wiſhes: but he here found a new trial of his virtue, where he hoped to have found a place of reſt and repoſe. This Abbey had lately loſt a great number of its members: and in order to adapt the ability of its ſubjects to the ſeverity of its Rules; the Superiors had judged it prudent not to admit any perſons as new members, but thoſe whoſe natural conſtitution was already abſolutely formed, and capable of obſerving the ſeverities of its Rule. Benedict arrived a ſhort time after this new regulation had been made. And it was not judged proper to diſpenſe with this rule, ſo ſoon after making it, in order to admit him to a tryal; and therefore he could not obtain admittance.

The regret which he experienced in conſequence of this refuſal cannot be expreſſed. He was ſtruck with a lively and pungent grief: but he bore it with the patience and reſignation becoming a true Chriſtian. But as the permiſſion which he had obtained from his parents particularly regarded his going to the Abbey of La Trappe, into which he could not then be received; he immediately returned again to his father's houſe, to wait with ſubmiſſion to the decrees of divine Providence, for a more favourable time to put his project in execution.

One

One of his Uncles who was then Vicar
of the Parish of Couteville, and Rector of
the Schools therein established, was desired
to continue his education, and perfect him
in the knowledge of the Latin tongue.

He here found in M. Vincent, all that
he had lost by the death of the worthy
Rector of Erin. The testimony which
the Right Rev. Bishop of Boulogne gives
of the virtues of M. Vincent, affords us an
opinion of him far greater than every other
eulogium*. This worthy Ecclesiastick already looked upon his nephew as a model
of virtue. He immediately loved him
with as much affection as if he was his
own son. And Benedict was not behind
hand with him, but afforded every motive
of consolation to his Uncle, by his docility

* " Sir, Among the letters which I send to
" you, there is one of Mr. Vincent, Uncle of
" the Venerable Benedict Joseph Labre. His
" testimony ought to make so much the more
" impression, as he is one of the most worthy
" Priests that I know. His extraordinary piety,
" his austere life, his generous and compassionate
" charity for the poor, have gained him the
" esteem and veneration of the publick to such a
" degree, that in places where he is known, he
" is already canonized by the voice of the people;
" for they commonly call him, not Mr. Vin-
" cent, but Saint Vincent." *Bishop of Boulogne's
Letter of June* 18, 1783.

lity and endeavours to profit by his in-
ftruſtions, and his example. The account
which M. Vincent himfelf gives of his pu-
pil, excufes our giving any other particular account of his conduct. It is fufficient
to tranfcribe a part of the Affidavit made
by this virtuous Prieft, who is now actually
Rector of the Parifh of la Peffe.

" Benedict Jofeph, fays he, rendered
" himfelf amiable from his moft tender
" years, on account of his great mildnefs,
" of which he has on many occafions
" given fignal proofs at Couteville, amongft
" fome ftudents whom I then taught.
" There was one, a very turbulent youth,
" who knowing him to be of a peaceful
" difpofition, ufed to make it his diverfion
" to thwart and mortify him: but he ne-
" ver refifted him either by words or ac-
" tions. He has exercifed his patience fo
" far, as that, rather than to refift, or
" make any complaints againft him, he has
" fuffered himfelf to be very much annoy-
" ed with the cold in winter.—I have ob-
" ferved in Benedict, a great deal of piety,
" and inclination to read good books.
" The works of Pere l'Aveugle have given
" him this inclination, and this ardent de-
" fire of leading a penitential life: he has
" read them feveral times: and as he had
" a found judgment, and a good memory,
" he has imprinted in his foul, the truths
" which he took notice of in thefe books."

Father

Father le Jeune had rendered himfelf famous by the Miffions which occupied his zeal during almoft the whole courfe of his life. The efteem which Benedict entertained for his works, would naturally excite in his foul a love for thofe Priefts who dedicated themfelves to this function, which is as laborious as it is refpectable. Some Miffionaries being come into the Diocefs of Boulogne, to begin their Preaching at Bocaval, Brias, Zoillecour, and Recéemats, the pious youth followed them in thefe different Parifhes: and thought of nothing but the falvation of his foul. Beholding the zeal which thefe Fathers (who were of the congregation of the Miffion eftablifhed by St. Vincent of Paul) demonftrated in endeavouring to convert finners from their evil ways and bring them to a life of virtue and holinefs; he applied to Mr. Chonault, who was one of that congregation, and at that time fuperior of the Seminary of Boulogne; and befought him to hear his General Confeffion, which was the *third* that he made in the courfe of his life.

Benedict, who every day fighed after folitude, and a place of retirement, was cut to the heart to find his hopes fo long delayed. Finding that his being under the proper age rendered him incapable of being admitted into La Trappe: he thought that he fhould not meet with fo many ſtacles if he ſolicited that favour at ſome Convent of Carthuſians. This he communicated to his Director: who approved of his deſign; and the pious youth returned to Amette to acquaint his parents with it, and to aſk their conſent to put it in execution.

CHAP. VIII.

The Servant of God meets with new obſtacles againſt his entering into a Religious State, both from his Parents and from the Carthuſians of Longueneſſe and Montreuil.

THE parents of Benedict having conſented to his following his inclination of embracing a Religious State in the Abbey of La Trappe; he had good reaſon to hope they would not oppoſe his inclination of entering into another order whoſe Rules were leſs ſevere. But in this he was miſtaken, for he found his parents oppoſed his entrance into a convent of Carthuſians no leſs than they had before oppoſed his going to La Trappe. They did not fail to repreſent to him the temporal advantages which he abandoned by ſuch a reſolution, the uncertainty of ſucceſs in his undertaking, the raſhneſs of embracing a ſtate of life which he might not be able to go through, the utility that he might be of to his family in aſſiſting his parents in the

F education

education of his brothers and fisters, and
what ought still more to touch him to the
heart, the love of his parents, and the affist-
ance and fupport which he might there-
after be able to afford them, in cafe they
fhould by any unforefeen misfortunes be
reduced to diftrefs, and every other motive
which could fhew how afflicting to them,
would be the feparation and facrifice which
he wanted to make of himfelf to God.

But the averfion which he entertained
againft the world, the defire of renouncing
all things for the fake of God, and that he
might live only for his fake, had taken fo
deep a root in the heart of the fervant of
God, as not to fuffer him to be fwayed by
worldly or human motives, or to fuffer his
refolution to be overcome by mere appear-
ances of good, or poffibilities of things
which were not likely to happen in effect.

At the fame time he met with another
obftacle which he before never thought
on, and which a fecond time rendered ufelefs the confent which he had obtained of
his Parents. For when he went to the
Convent of Carthufians at Montreuil, the
Prior received him with good nature and
affability, fpoke to him with cordiality, and
gave proofs of his efteem and affection
for him; but finifhed his converfation by
objecting to his youth, and by telling him
that fuch was the cuftom of the houfe that
he could not be admitted till he had ftudied
Philofophy

Philofophy at leaft for the fpace of one year, and likewife had learned the Gregorian mufick called Plain Song. But to comfort him, he added, that as foon as ever he was qualified in·thofe two things, he would receive him with pleafure. Benedict expreffed his gratitude for this obliging promife made to him by the Prior, and left Montreuil with intent to return to his Parents, but he was informed that the Convent of the Carthufians at Longuenefs was a houfe wherein he might in all likelihood be received with greater facility. The Servant of God, in confequence of this information went to Longuenefs, and the fuccefs which he here met with anfwered his wifhes. The Prior gave him a favourable reception, and admitted him to the exercifes of the Novicefhip.

This Epoch of the life of the Servant of God, for thofe fouls whom God calls to a ·ftate of extraordinary perfection, is a fource of great inftruction: it was one of the hardeft tryals he ever experienced: for corporal aufterities are nothing when compared to the anguifh of the foul. This folitude which had been the object he had fo long fighed after, into which he at once rufhed with fo much ardour and fo much joy, this folitude which he had looked upon as a true land of promife, he foon found to be a land of trouble and affliction, a dry and barren defart.

F 2

The

The masters of an internal and spiritual life know, and they only can well describe that state of obscurity, and sometimes of terrors and anguish, by which God frequently conducts those souls which he destines to attain to a high degree of perfection. This is one of the means which his divine providence makes use of, to lay in chosen souls the deep foundations of humility, to make them die to themselves, to divest themselves of all confidence in themselves or others, that he may afterwards attach them closely to himself by the means of contemplation and love.

The soul which entertains an ardent love, tends always to an union with the object of its love : and it is by the means of contemplation, that love conducts the soul to an union with its beloved object.

The first grace which moves the souls of Christians called to a state of perfection, is a ray of divine light which reveals to them the knowledge of God, and the knowledge of themselves. Employed in the contemplation of these two things, the soul is soon convinced, that God is the being of beings, and the creature a mere nothing : it sees on one hand the immensity of God's greatness, and on the other the abyss of its own wretchedness; an immense sanctity, and an abyss of sin : an immense love, and an abyss of ingratitude.

It

It is in this manner that the Soul compares what is finite, with what is infinite: the enormity of fin, with the idea which it forms of the infinite holiness of God: the punishment of the finner, with the infinite justice of God: the ingratitude, or little love which men entertain in their hearts for God; with the infinite charity of God for men: the negligent manner in which they ordinarily perform their duties to their Creator, with the perfection with which his Law requires they should be performed: the fevere account which they muft one day render of their actions, with the infinite number of the graces and favours they have received from God: and the weaknefs and infufficiency of their repentance with the multitude of their offences and imperfections.

But the eye of the Soul, which is the underftanding, cannot remain long fixed on the contemplation of this double abyfs of the greatnefs of God, and the wretchednefs of man; it cannot embrace at once, the infinite diftance there is between God and the finner, and bring both thefe objects into one point of view, without being immediately overwhelmed with anguifh and confufion. Struck with aftonifhment, at the contemplation of the divine perfections, and its own imperfections; the Soul perceives nothing in itfelf but fpots, ftains, filthinefs, coldnefs, ingratitude and

weak-

weakneſs. God at that time ſeems to withdraw himſelf from the Soul, and permits that it ſhould be for a time given up to fears and terrors.

The Soul being then oppreſſed with theſe reflections, opreſſes itſelf ſtill more; ſorrow, dryneſs and diſguſt, baniſh all ſenſible ſatisfactions from the Soul. The more it dwells on theſe reflections, and thinks that it cannot eſcape the wrath of God, ſo much the more it loves God, without being ſenſible that it loves him: and by how much greater is the horror which it entertains for ſin, ſo much the more does it perſuade itſelf that it is infected with it.

Then it is that a kind of ſpiritual darkneſs ſpreads itſelf over the Soul and obſcures the underſtanding. God whoſe very nature is mercy, appears then only as a God of infinite juſtice. A God who is infinitely amiable, appears to be a God of ſeverity, terrors, and vengeance. A God who is always ready to pardon penitent ſinners, appears as a God who is ready to puniſh them for their crimes. And a God who makes uſe of this ſubtraction of conſolation only as a means to prove the humility and fidelity of his ſervants, appears as a God who caſts off and abandons them.

Theſe terrors paſs from the imagination into the heart of a man: the ſtorms of trouble and anxiety begin to arriſe, the terrors of eternity make a deep impreſſion

on

on his Soul: all his thoughts feem to be full of horrors, defolation, and anguifh; and all his ftrength being exhaufted by thefe terrors and apprehenfions, the Soul feems to fall into a kind of agony. But in this very moment, when he thinks himfelf upon the very brink of everlafting perdition; the trial ceafes: God diffipates the clouds of darknefs, reftores a calm, and affords peace, comfort, and ftrength, to the afflicted Soul.

It is in this manner that Jefus Chrift has made thofe chofen fouls to drink of the chalice of the fufferings which he endured in the garden of Olives, whom he afterwards conducted to Mount Calvary, that they might die with him, and be crucified to the world, and the world to them. It was by this hard, this fevere, but falutary proof of their fidelity, that God conducted Job, David, and Jeremias; and in thefe latter ages S. Terefa, S. Ignatius of Loyola, and S. Francis of Sales.

Benedict Jofeph was called to pafs fucceffively through thefe different ftates of the interiour and fpiritual life, and to arrive at an union with God by the means of Prayer and Contemplation. It was therefore according to the ordinary difpofition which Providence had decreed for the progrefs of Souls called to perfection, that he underwent this trial: his Faith and fubmiffion to the will of God had already been

exercifed

exercifed for fome years, and was one of the principal means which God made ufe of to ground him well in humility, and to augment his inclination to the aufterities of a penitential and mortified life.

It is principally to this caufe that his departure from the Carthufian Convent of Longueneffe is to be attributed. For notwithftanding the rigorous exactnefs with which the Rule of S. Bruno is obferved in that houfe: it appeared ftill too mild and eafy to this humble Penitent; who fmitten with the fear of the judgments of God, and reckoning himfelf one of the greateft of finners; imagined he fhould not be able to fave his Soul, unlefs he embraced an order more auftere. Poffibly alfo a fedentary life, and fuch a profound retirement, did not fuit his conftitution and difpofition, which was naturally lively and active. Be that as it may, the interiour anguifh which he experienced, and the hopes of one day obtaining his admiffion into the Abbey of La Trappe, renewed all his former ideas and affection for that Houfe, and inclined him to think that God had not called him to make his Religious Profeffion in this of Longueneffe. He therefore left it after having gone through fix weeks of his Novicefhip.

His firft care was to go and relate all that had paffed to his Confeffor, to give him an account of the little fuccefs he had

experi-

experienced, in his attempt, and of the
state of his dejected and afflicted Soul.
The zealous Director who was well experienced in the ways of God, and in the
direction of Souls, soon delivered him
from his troubles and anxieties, and restored him to peace of mind: and advised
him to return to his Father's house, and
their wait for whatever Providence might
be pleased to ordain concerning him, and
put it in execution.

CHAP. IX.

*The Servant of God returns to Amette, and
experiences new oppositions for the space
of Two Years.*

IT is said that victory always increases
both our strength and our courage.
This was verified in this Servant of God,
who having surmounted the temptations
with which he had been so violently agitated; after this storm had happily sub-
sided, found that he was able to do all
things through him who strengthened
him. For the new trials which he soon
after had to undergo, will shew how necessary for him was his confidence in God,
and that firmness and resolution of Soul
which was the effect of that confidence.

Although he had quitted the Cloister,
he nevertheless thought himself called by
God

God to a life of poverty and mortification. This was evidently his vocation. He never entertained a doubt of it: and therefore though he had returned to his Parents, he took a refolution of living according to it, by every means that was in his power. For this reafon, he immediately began to add extraordinary works of mortification to his fafts and prayers. His Mother whofe tendernefs and affection for him, rendered her more and more vigilant and attentive to him, foon perceived it, and made great complaints againft it. She many times found that inftead of fleeping in his bed, he had paffed whole nights laying on the chamber floor. She dreaded the effects of this kind of mortification, and exclaimed againft a kind of fervour of penance which fhe looked upon as unreafonable, indifcreet, and likely to prejudice his health. The anfwer which he gave to his Mother when fhe repremanded him for it, was modeft and full of refpect; but fhewed him to be ftill firm, and unfhaken in his refolution: " God faid he, " calls me to lead a penitent and mortified " life: and it is proper that I fhould begin " to fulfill his Divine will."

His refolution of following his vocation to a penitential life, was fo fteady and unfhaken, that when his Mother one day refufed to confent to his leaving her houfe, through fear that when once he was gone,

–he

he might not be able to find means of support; he without any hesitation said to her: " Let me go, Mother, I will live upon " roots as the Anchorets formerly did; " for, by the grace of God, we are still " able to live in the same manner as they " did."

These fears and complaints of his mother were not long kept secret. She made no doubt, but that by engaging several others to take her part, she should be more likely to bring him to compliance; and shake that resolution of her Son, which had filled her soul with astonishment.

Hence it was, that neighbours, friends, and almost all the family, out of a good intention joined together, to raise a kind of persecution against him, in order if possible to make him abandon his projects. They continually blamed his pretended obstinacy in troubling, afflicting, and alarming a family, for which he ought to entertain the greatest gratitude and affection. They represented to him the inutility of so many steps he had already taken, and journeys and trials which he had already made, and which having all tended to nothing, but to increase the expences of his education, rendered his alledged vocation suspicious. And sometimes making use of bitter reproaches they endeavoured to deject, and deter him, by severe and stinging expressions.

But

But this is always a weak method of attempting to overcome the conſtancy of a man who is ſincerely humble. Although Benedict was always ſubmiſſive and obedient to his parents in every thing which did not claſh with his vocation, yet he thought that his fidelity in following the inſpiration of God, was not yet any ways detrimental to the love and reſpect which he entertained for, and was due to his parents: wherefore being full of confidence in the perſuaſion, that his firſt duty was to follow the call of God, he was calm in the midſt of the tempeſt that ſurrounded him, and never failed to preſerve the good humour, and even the gaiety, that was natural to him.

God gave a bleſſing to this conſtancy and humility by changing the views and diſpoſitions of his parents. For being perſuaded that a longer reſiſtance would only ſerve to afflict their Son, whom they loved, and whoſe virtue they reſpected; they reſolved to facilitate the execution of his pious deſigns.

CHAP.

CHAP. X.

He applys himself to the study of Philoso-
phy and Church Musick. His conduct
while he was with M. Dufour, who was
then Vicar of Ligni, and is now Rector
of Anchi-aux-Bois.

BENEDICT having attained to the
twentieth year of his age, thought
that it was necessary to fix himself in some
state of life, and free his parents from any
further care or expence on account of his
education. His heart always sighed after
the Abbey of La Trappe: his desire of
leading a penitential and mortified life,
made him prefer that, to every other retreat : but a holy impatience for dedicating
himself without delay to the service of
God, and his situation with regard to his
parents, did not permit him to wait till
the age at which he might be received into that House.

His interiour troubles and anxieties had
moreover again returned and agitated his
Soul. Benedict who was humble and
mortified, who had passed the time of his
youth in retirement, prayer, fasting, and a
renunciation of sensual pleasures ; still perceived himself penetrated with a lively
fear of the judgments of God, and looked
upon himself as a sinner deserving of hatred

G

and contempt: nay he considered even
his very imperfections, as sins of which he
could not hope for pardon, but only on
condition of giving up his body to undergo
a rigorous penance during the whole course
of his life. He looked upon himself as
out of his element, so long as he was not
in some austere place of retirement; and
he considered as lost to eternity, all the
time that he should voluntarily continue in
the world.

The promise that had been made to him
by the Prior of the Carthusians at Montreuil, of receiving him as soon as he
should have learned Logick and Church
Musick, made him desire to be in a capacity of fulfilling these two conditions. In
consequence of this desire he applied to
M. Dufour who was then Vicar of the
Parish of Ligni, and afterwards Rector of
that of Anchi-aux-Bois, who undertook to
instruct him in these two Sciences. The
Master charmed with the virtues and good
qualities of the disciple which Providence
had directed to him, treated him rather
like a Friend than a Scholar: and gave
him an entire liberty to follow the plan of
conduct, and the exercises of Piety which
he had prescribed for himself.

The study of Church Musick was very
agreeable to his inclination, on account of
the relation it had to the worship of God;
for which reason the young man applied
himself

himfelf to it with diligence, and with pleafure.

But it was not fo with regard to Logick. He immediately perceived how little inclination and difpofition he had for this Science. Notwithftanding all the endeavours of his mafter, to explain to him every thing that was difficult in it; notwithftanding all the efforts which he himfelf made ufe of, to correfpond with the good will of his Mafter; he was never able to conquer the repugnance which he experienced in himfelf whenever he was to apply himfelf to this branch of ftudy. Neverthelefs he foon arrived at a condition of being able to pafs the examinations which he had to undergo: but this was not fo much owing to his application, as to a certain kind of facility of comprehenfion, which was natural to him.

Benedict remained three months with M. Dufour, dividing his time almoft entirely, between prayer, and reading; nourifhing his piety by fafting, penitential exercifes, and a privation of all, even innocent pleafures. For being then arrived at an age wherein it was permitted him to lay down a plan for his own conduct; he made it a law for himfelf abfolutely to abftain from them. From that time, no one could prevail upon him to be prefent at the recreations, which on Sundays and Holidays, are in ufe in the Country Parifhes,

after

after the Evening Service of the Church is finished.

One of his Fellow Students once entertained an idea, that he should be able to make him break through this plan of conduct, and bring him to the place of these publick recreations: in order to this, he urged every argument which his genius could suggest, to persuade him, and obtain of him to go at least for once, and out of complaisance: but all his endeavours proved unsuccessful, and the servant of God continued faithful to the law which he had made for his own conduct.

As soon as ever he found himself sufficiently instructed in Church Musick and Logick, he immediately, and without a moment's delay, set out for the Convent of Montreuil, and begged the favour of being received into that House.

CHAP. XI.

He arrives at Montreuil, and continues some time in that House, in quality of a Postulant.

THE Prior of Montreuil being assured that Benedict had sufficiently complied with the conditions which he had required of him: made no difficulty to receive him into his House, to try his vocation for a time in quality of a Postulant,

before

before he fhould admit him to the Habit
of the Order. The folitude of Montreuil,
immediately afforded Benedict a pleafure
and fatisfaction, like to that of a victorious
General after he has fuftained a long,
a violent, and dubious combat: or to that
of a man, who after a long and earneft
purfuit of riches and honours, at length
finds his endeavours crowned with fuccefs.
The aufterities of the Rule, the length of
the Divine Offices, the nightly Vigils, the
variety of the exercifes which fucceeded
one another without interruption, occupied at firft, all the activity of his zeal;
and he here found reading, prayer, retirement, and penitential exercifes, fufficient
to fatisfy all the defires of his Soul. A
fenfible joy which fhewed itfelf in his countenance, indicated the peace of his mind,
and the content of his heart. This comfort rendered him ftill more fervent, by a
fcrupulous affiduity in the difcharge of his
duties, and of all the obfervances of the
Houfe. But this calm was of fhort dura-
tion. New tempefts began to arrife: and
it was from his own fervour, that trouble
and uneafinefs began again to take place in
his mind.

Benedict immediately gave himfelf up to
follow his inclination to meditation, and
took for the ordinary fubject of his thoughts,
the infinite holinefs of God, the greatnefs
of his obligations towards God, and the

multitude

multitude of the graces and favours which
he had received fiom him. His imagination was lively, and his confcience was delicate and timorous: and as the eye which
has been for a long time fixed on the daz-
zling fplendor of the meridian Sun, in the
moment when it turns again to view the
things on the earth, perceives nothing but
a kind of confufed darknefs: fo it was with
Benedict, who being employed in medi-
tating on the infinite holinefs and the infinite goodnefs of God, on the perfection
and purity of his law, and on the greatnefs
of his love for man: when he afterwards
came to take a view of his own foul, he
faw nothing in it but ftains, but ingratitude, and fubjects of fear and terror. The
fame truths, the fame interiour anguifh
which he had experienced at Longueneffe,
afflicted him again. The Rule of St. Bruno
appeared to him to have been made only
for Solitaries who had preferved their Bap-
tifmal Innocence: but he thought it far too
mild for fuch a finner as he looked upon
himfelf to be.

His body foon began to feel the effects
of this agitation and uneafinefs of mind:
and he was too lively to conceal it for any
long time. The good Religious perceived
it: they pitied, confoled, and endeavoured
to encourage the pious young man to put
his truft and confidence in God: but, thinking that he was not defigned by God to
embrace

embrace their Inſtitute, they adviſed him to leave their Houſe. And accordingly, after ſix week's trial, he left it on the ſecond of October, 1769.—

On the ſame day he wrote a letter to his parents, to acquaint them with his departure from it. His letter which is an edifying monument of his piety, deſcribes, far better than we ſhould be able to do, both the livelineſs of his faith and the goodneſs of his heart. It is as follows:

Letter of the Servant of God to his Parents.

" My dear Father and Mother.

" This is to acquaint you that the Car-
" thuſians having judged me not a proper
" perſon for their ſtate of life, I quitted
" their houſe on the ſecond day of Octo-
" ber. I look upon this as an order of di-
" vine Providence which calls me to a ſtill
" more perfect ſtate. They themſelves
" have told me that it is the hand of God
" which has withdrawn me from remain-
" ing with them. I now intend to go to
" La Trappe, the place which I have ſo
" long, and ſo earneſtly deſired. I beg
" your pardon for all my diſobediences, and
" for all the uneaſineſs which I have at
" any time given you. I beg that both of
" you will give me your bleſſing, that the
" Lord may accompany me. I will not
" fail to pray to our good God for you all
" the

CHAP. XII.

*He goes from Montreuil to La Trappe, and
from thence to the Abbey of Sept-Fonts,
where he is admitted. The time of his
continuing there, and his departure from
this last Monastery.*

GOD preserved his Servant from des-
pondency, by always permitting him
to hope, that at La Trappe he should at
length find a place of retreat and rest.
His humility, which made him look upon
himself as a sinner, who is under a necef-
sity of doing great penance for his sins; inclined him to think that he should not be
able to save his Soul, unless he embraced
that Religious Order which was of all the
most austere. On the other hand his confidence in God, whom he looked on as a
God of infinite mercy, and who desires not
that any sinner should perish; would not
permit him to doubt but that if he persevered, God would be pleased to grant his
desires. The Rule of the Order of La
Trappe was the most rigid of any that he
knew; he was therefore in a manner
assured that God, who had proportioned
every thing according to the wants of his
creatures, had provided this solitary re-
source for the relief of great sinners. And
being animated with this comfortable reflection,

flection, he set out a second time, and made all possible haste towards La Trappe.

But God had prepared a new trial of his Servant's humility and perseverance by a new refusal: he presented himself a second time for admittance, but presented himself in vain. The gate of this retreat therefore was from that time for ever shut against him.

But God never permits any man to be tempted beyond what he is able to endure. The Servant of God being firm in this persuasion, and entertaining in his Soul an unshaken confidence in the Divine Goodness, like Abraham hoped against all hope. Sept-Fonts was the place which now remained for him to try wherein to get admittance. And notwithstanding the excessive fatigue which he had undergone, the length of the journey, and the continual rains, which had made the roads almost impassable: he departed a second time from La Trappe, and arrived at Sept-Fonts so soon, that on the 28th of October he was admitted to take the Habit of a Choir Novice by the name of Brother Urban.

He would not have preferred the Abbey of La Trappe, but only because he thought that the Rule of Sept-Fonts was too mild. But he was very happy, and looked upon the refusal of his admission into that House as the effect of a particular

cular mercy of God in his favour, when he found that the Monastery of Sept-Fonts was in no respect behind hand with that of La Trappe: but on the contrary, that in many things it even surpassed it in austerity and strictness of discipline.

He passed eight months in the exercises of the noviceship: he was pious, obedient and laborious, and discharged every duty with punctuality and an exactness proceeding from an holy emulation: but the interiour troubles and anguish which he had before experienced, returning again; a two months sickness which had exhausted all his strength; and the well grounded fears which his Superiors entertained, that being of a weak constitution, his zeal surpassed his corporal abilities, and that he had not sufficient strength to endure the austerities of their Institute: all concurred to manifest, what was the will of God, who had permitted such invincible obstacles to be opposed to his desires.

On the second of July 1770, he quitted the Monastery of Sept-Fonts, and now resolved to go to Italy, in hopes of being there admitted into one of the like kind of Monasteries, where he was informed the lives of the Religious were very regular, and the rules very austere.

Let us now stop, and make a few moments reflection on him, and his situation, at this important period. If we consider
him

him according to our ordinary way of judging of things, his situation will appear to be truly diſtreſſing and afflicting. How many ſteps had he taken, and how many labours had he undergone apparently in vain! The long and ardent wiſhes which he had entertained from his moſt tender age, and which every day increaſed more and more, the nature of his diſpoſitions, his inclinations, and his virtues: the plan of his ſtudies, and of his exerciſes of piety, conſtantly directed and tending to this point; the fervour and perſeverance of the prayers which he offered up to God in order to know his vocation: the expences of an education prolonged beyond the uſual term: and in a word the whole life of Benedict even from his infancy had always been a preparation for a Religious ſtate, and a kind of a continual Noviceſhip. This was the precious pearl to purchaſe which he had ſold all that he had; he had relinquiſhed his patrimony; refiſted the wiſhes, and gained victories over the tenderneſs of his parents, which at the ſame time cut him to the heart. And nevertheleſs he appears to be now reduced to a ſituation, in which he ſeems to know not what to do, or whither to go. Yet this was the ſituation in which he found himſelf at twenty-two years of age, after having made ſo many journeys, gone through ſo many fatigues and labours, relinquiſhed all that he

had, or had reason to expect, and made so
many attempts to be admitted to a Religious state.

Having a long time before quitted his
Father's house, he could not even think of
returning to it again. He feared that such
a step would be a kind of injustice, by making himself a burden to a family already
tired with the great expences they had
been at on his account. His health being
impaired, and his constitution weakened,
he was little fit for the Cloister, and still
less fit for the world: he was destitute of
the means of getting a livelihood, destitute
of support, of a friend to help him, or of
an earthly comfort: and at the same time
overwhelmed with fears and anguish of
mind. This is a faithful representation of
his situation at that time. But why should
we fear for the just man whom God purifies in the furnace of afflictions. God
tries the just, but he never abandons them:
and his divine Providence watches over his
Elect with a particular care, even at the
very time when he seems to have forsaken
them. It was therefore from the very
source, and in the very height of his troubles, that God was pleased to make peace
to arise, and shine upon him: and sent him
a ray of comfort, which thenceforward never ceased to direct and fix him in that
state of life to which he called him.

During

During the whole course of his life he had endeavoured to know and to fulfil the will of God: and we may say that this was the only object he had in view. From this moment therefore he began to know what was the will of God in his regard: and from this moment he began to be happy. He was now persuaded in his own mind, that if it was not the will of God that he should enter into a Monastick State; at least it was his divine will that he should, even remaining in the world, practise that renunciation of the world, that interiour solitude and recollection, that self-denial, that life of prayer, that poverty, the penitential austerities and every other virtue which is practised by those who are engaged in a Monastick state.

In order to put him in a way of following the extraordinary vocation to which God called him, it was highly proper to furnish him with able masters, with instructions, with examples, and with patterns for his imitation, and in order to procure these advantages for him, God had conducted him into different places of religious retirement. And as Benedict had actually found all these things united in the different Monasteries into which he had been received: he looked upon this disposition of Divine Providence, as a singular favour which deserved to be repaid with the utmost gratitude of his heart.

Benedict

Benedict being now perfuaded of what were the defigns of God concerning him, now gave himfelf no farther uneafinefs concerning the means which God would make ufe of to accomplifh what he had ordained: he therefore refigned himfelf up without referve to the difpofition of his divine Providence: refolved to follow the conduct, the light, and infpirations of his Holy Spirit; and to fubmit himfelf to all the fufferings and afflictions which might await him; without afking, or defiring any thing, but to carry the Crofs, and to drink of the Chalice of the fufferings of his Divine Redeemer.

It is therefore in this new carreer of merits and virtues, which we have now to confider this Servant of God.

CHAP. XIII.

Pilgrimages undertaken by Benedict Joseph Labre.

ALL men are called upon to lead a good and holy life, as a means to obtain everlafting happinefs. And as in the *houfe of God there are many manfions,* fo likewife there are different ways of arriving at it. For befides the common and ordinary roads to heaven, there are fome which are extraordinary, and fome fingular: but it would be great rafhnefs to attempt to go

by

by thefe without evident figns of divine
infpiration, and of a vocation to them
which has been maturely confidered, and
examined. I am now going to fpeak of
the devotion known by the name of Pilgrimages, in which this Servant of God fpent
a great part of his life: and in which he
behaved in fuch manner, as leaves no
room to doubt, that which would be for
the generality of Chriftians a temptation to
remiffnefs and diffipation, was to him a
means of increafing his merits, an exercife of penance, and a means of promoting
the fanctification of his Soul.

Without doubt as foon as he found himfelf in the particular circumftances in
which he was when he quitted the Abbey
of Sept-Fonts: at a diftance from the place
of his birth, difengaged from the world and
all that was in it, and finding his defign of
confecrating himfelf to God in a Monaftick
State oppofed by innumerable obftacles:
his love of humility, poverty, and a penitential life, prefented to his zealous mind
the practife of that kind of piety which he
afterwards put in execution.

Rome, which is the Capital and only
Centre of the Catholick Church; a place
rendered facred by the triumphs and the
Tombs of the glorious Apoftles S. Peter
and S. Paul: and fo famous for its monu-
ments of Religion and the fpiritual trea-
fures which it enjoys and difpences to the
H 3   Faithful;

Faithful; was the principal place and object of the Pilgrimages of this Servant of
God. Wherefore from the moment of
his departure from the Abbey of Sept-
Fonts in 1770, he formed in his mind a refolution to make a journey thither; and immediately began to put it in execution.

Being arrived at Guiers in Piedmont,
he wrote a letter to his father and mother,
acquainting them with the reafon which
hindered him from remaining all his life
in that Monaftery. That letter contained
in fome fort his laft farewell to his family:
and indeed from that time his parents never received any account of him till after
his death.

*The following is a Copy of the Second and
laft Letter which he fent to his Parents.*

" My Dear Father and Mother,
" You have heard that I have left the
" Abbey of Sept-Fonts, and without doubt
" you are uneafy and defirous to know
" what rout I have taken, and what kind
" of life I intend to take to. It is to dif-
" charge my duty in this regard, and to re-
" move your uneafinefs, that I now write
" to you. I muft therefore acquaint you
" that I left Sept-Fonts on the fecond of
" July: I had a fever when I came out of
" Sept-Fonts, which left me on the fourth
" day after, and I am now going to Rome.
                                 " I have

" I have now got almoſt half way thither.
" I have not travelled very faſt ſince I left
" Sept-Fonts, on account of the exceſſive
" hot weather which there always is in the
" month of Auguſt in Piedmont, where I
" now am, and where I have been on ac-
" count of a little complaint, detained for
" the ſpace of three weeks in an Hoſpital
" where I was kindly treated. In other
" reſpects I have been very well ſince I left
" Sept-Fonts. There are in Italy many
" Monaſteries where the Religious live
" very regular and auſtere lives, I deſign
" to enter into one of them, and I hope
" that God will proſper my deſign. I
" know that there is one of thoſe Mona-
" ſteries of the order of La Trappe, the
" Abbot of which has wrote to an Abbot in
" France, acquainting him that if any
" Frenchmen have a mind to go thither,
" he will receive them, becauſe he is in
" want of Subjects. I have taken out
" very good Certificates from Sept-Fonts.
" Do not make yourſelves uneaſy on my
" account. I will not fail to write to you
" from time to time. And I ſhall be glad
" to hear of you and of my brothers and
" ſiſters : but this is not poſſible at preſent,
" becauſe I am not yet ſettled in any
" fixed place. I will not fail to pray for
" you every day. I beg you will pardon
" me for all the uneaſineſſes that I have
" given you ; and that you will give me
                                   " your

" your blesfing, that God may favour my
" defigns. It is by the order of Provi-
" dence that I undertake the journey which
" I now make. Labour diligently for the
" falvation of your Souls, and take care of
" the education of my brothers and fifters.
" Watch over their conduct; and medi-
" tate on the eternal torments of Hell, and
" on the fmall number of the Elect. I am
" very happy with my having undertaken
" my prefent journey. I beg you will
" give my compliments to my grand-mo-
" ther, my grand father, my aunts, to my
" brother James, to all my brothers and
" fifters, and to my uncle Chois-Francis.
" I am going into a country which is a good
" country for travellers. I am obliged to
" pay the poftage of this to France.——
" Again afking your blefsing, and your
" pardon for all the uneafinefses that I
" have given you, I fubfcribe myfelf,
" *Roziers* in *Piedmont*,   Your moft
"   . 31, 1770.   affectionate Son,
          " Benedict Jofeph Labre."

From Piedmont he with a truly edifying
piety vifited all the Churches which lay in
his way to Loretto, where he arrived in
the month of November: his tender devotion to the Blefsed Virgin, whom he looked on as his mother, and the great favours
he had received from God, which he confidered as obtained by her intercefsion:
                                        made

made him entertain a very particular affection and predilection for this famous place all the reft of his life.

After this he went to Affifium which is famous for being the birth place of S. Francis. Here he performed his devotions, and was admitted into the Confraternity eftablifhed in this place in honour of that Saint: and according to cuftom received a fmall bleffed Cord which he conftantly wore, and which was found about him when his cloaths was taken off from him after his death.

Being arrived at Rome the firft time in the beginning of December, he was for three days admitted into the Hofpital of St. Louis which is there eftablifhed for the reception of French Pilgrims.

Rome without doubt prefents a profpect capable of enkindling a lively devotion in any truly Religious Soul: but it would be neceffary to be animated with the fpirit of Benedict Jofeph Labre, to be able to defcribe the lively fentiments of piety which he experienced, the fervour of devotion with which he vifited all the holy places, the effufions of gratitude and love for Jefus Chrift and his bleffed Mother, and the tears of compunction, of fenfibility, and joy which he fhed in the prefence of the Tomb of the holy Apoftles.

After remaining between eight and nine months principally in Rome, he undertook

a fecond

a fecond journey to Loretto, where he arrived about the middle of September 1771.

In the preceding month of June he had
been to Fabriano, to vifit the tomb of
S. Romuauld, founder of the Order of
Camaldulences, and who had been famous
for his great virtues, but particularly for a
long practice of extraordionary aufterities.

He paffed fifteen days in this place of
devotion, where he was more and more
confirmed in his refolution, of paffing his
life in a ftate of rigorous poverty and penance. And it was in confequence of this
refolution, and to purify his foul from all
affection to fin, that he defired for the
third time to make a general Confeffion.
M. Pagetti, Rector of Fabriano to whom
he applied for that purpofe, in this manner
relates this particular of his life.

" The pious Pilgrim having come into
" the Sacrifty to look for me after the
" Mafs was finifhed, earneftly defired I
" would do him the favour to hear his
" general confeffion at any time when I
" fhould be at leifure. I could not refufe him
" that comfort, after that he had fhewn
" fo great a defire of it. Two or three
" days after this, going to the Church
" with this intention, and finding that he
" had properly prepared himfelf for it, I
" heard his confeffion which he made
" of his whole life beginning from the
" day in which he made his confeffion to me,
" and,

" and, going back from one period of
" time to another, till he came to his
" moft tender youth. In his Confeffion
" I admired the goodnefs of God, and the
" graces with which he had favoured him ;
" as well as his conftant fidelity in corre-
" fponding with thofe graces in every age
" of his life, in fpite of the artifices and
" fnares of the devil, and the temptations
" to which he had been expofed.

" Such was his humility, that he looked
" upon the graces and favours which he
" had received from Heaven, as only the
" effects of his own imagination. The
" Servant of God acquainted me with his
" defign of going to Compoftelia to vifit
" the body of St James, in whofe inter-
" ceffion he repofed a particular confi-
" dence. I obferved in him a fervent de-
" votion to the adorable Humanity of
" Jefus Chrift, and to his holy Mother,
" and a great compaffion for the Souls in
" Purgatory. To a great humility and
" a fingular contempt of his own body,
" which he called his carcafe, he joined an
" unbounded charity for his neighbour:
" whom he affifted to the utmoft of his
" power in a fpiritual way, by continually
" offering his moft fervent prayers to God
" for the converfion and Salvation of fin-
" ners: and though he was poor himfelf,
" he gave all that he had in alms, to
" the poor, referving for himfelf only the
" fmalleft

" fmalleft portion, of what was given to
" him, and fuch as was fcarce fufficient for
" his fupport for the prefent day without
" keeping any thing for the morrow."

Such was the conduct of this pious Pilgrim at Fabriano, and to which he conftantly adhered from the time in which God inclined him to follow this kind of life.

M. Pagetti adds that the inhabitants of Fabriano being ftruck with his poor appearance and his piety, immediately began to look on him as a Saint: and that as foon as he perceived they entertained a good opinion of him, his humility made him quit this part of the country, in order to avoid the marks of efteem and veneration which they fhewed him.

In the fame year 1771, he went to vifit the moft renowned places of devotion in the kingdom of Naples, which were, the Church of S. Nicholas, Bifhop of Myra at Barri: the Church of S. Januarius at Naples: the Church of S. Michael at Mount Gargano; and a great number of others.

The Servant of God was again at Naples on the 13th of February 1772, from whence he departed to return to Rome: where he remained till the month of June, which was the time when he went again to Loretto.

There

There is hardly any famous place of devotion in Europe which has not been visited by this Servant of God. In the year 1773, he was in Tuscany where he made another general Confession, which was the fourth he made in his life. There is no particular account of this journey: but there is no doubt but that his veneration for S. Francis induced him to visit the celebrated Church of that Saint, situated in the Mountains of Alvernia.

From the Register of those who have been received in the French Hospital of St. Louis, we learn that he was at Rome about Easter, in the year 1774. He must then have remained but a little time in this city: for in the month of December of the same year he was at Burgundy in France.

His devotion to the Blessed Virgin excited in his soul an indefatigable zeal which spurred him on to visit every place that was famous for her veneration.

The winter season which was then at its height, the great distance of the places, the severity of the cold, the asperity of the mountains which were covered with ice and snow, were not sufficient to hinder him from putting in execution a resolution he had entertained of leaving Burgundy, to go to Switzerland to visit the Church of our Lady of the Hermits at Einsilden, at which he arrived in the month of February.

I

This

This Church which is very rich and magnificently ornamented, belongs to a Convent of Benedictins, situated in the Diocese of Constance, about five leagues from the City of Sufa, which is the capital of the Canton of that name. Fourteen successive Popes have granted or confirmed considerable Privileges to that Monastery. And Benedict always entertained a particular veneration for this place, which is famous for the great concourse of Pilgrims who go thither from all parts of the world.

From Einsilden he went to visit some part of Germany, and in particular Waltshut, Hoggenschvyl, Walweil, and then went to Lucerne, from whence he returned again to Einsilden, where he remained till the beginning of July.

The circumstance of the Jubilee of the year 1775, induced him to go from Einsilden to Rome, where he continued during the remainder of that holy year.

In the month of February 1776, he for the fifth time made a Pilgrimage to Loretto. He set out notwithstanding it was then the depth of winter: and he undertook his third journey to Einsilden, which he happily accomplished: and in the course of that rout he again visited several of the famous places of devotion in Germany: particularly that of Waltshut upon the Rhine, where he was on the 20th of August 1776.

His

His return to Rome in the same year finished all his pious circumambulations: and for the remainder of his life he took up his residence in that capital: from whence he did not depart, but only to go once every year to pass a few days at Loretto, to render to the Blessed Virgin in her own house which she inhabited on earth, his annual tribute of gratitude and love.

After having given an account of the different journeys of this pious Pilgrim, it cannot be improper to make a few reflections on the merit of Pilgrimages, which we borrow from M. Alegiani. They certainly have been practised by a great number of holy persons. The illustrious Author of the Book entitled the Imitation of Jesus Christ, says with a great deal of truth; that those who give themselves up to a wandering life, very seldom become more holy. And in reality if we consider the life of Pilgrims in a certain light; we shall find that they are exposed to a thousand risks, and a thousand spiritual dangers, on account of the variety of persons with whom they meet, and the places through which they pass, and where they stop. They expose their mind to the danger of distractions, of curiosity, and of the search after novelties: all which are things which either extinguish the fervour of devotion or at least considerably weaken it.

But

But if Pilgrimages are looked on in another point of view, it cannot be denied that the life of a Pilgrim may be a means of fanctifying his foul : becaufe it perfectly difengages him from all attachment to the conveniences of this world which he might enjoy by refiding in a fixed place.

Who is there that is not acquainted with this Evangelical maxim : that by how much more the foul is difengaged from the things of this world; fo much more it is raifed towards Heaven ? To which we may add this confideration that the very places themfelves, the Tombs of the Saints which they go to vifit, naturally infpire them with certain fentiments of veneration, which at the fame time, excites in their Souls a confidence of obtaining from God by their interceffion, the graces and favours of which they ftand in need, and for which they petition.

- If Pilgrimages thus, confidered in themfelves may contribute to the Sanctification of thofe who undertake them, what may we not fay of thofe of Benedict who abandoning his country, expofing his health to danger, and renouncing the conveniencies of life, undertook this kind of penitential life, and travelled alone, unknown, on foot, and without provifion for his journeys; accompanied only by his virtues: fuffering by the heat of the fun, the feverity of the cold, the other inclemen-

cies

cies of the weather, and by a thousand other inconveniences and dangers inseparable from those kinds of journeys.

Some facts relative to these Pilgrimages give us to understand how, great was his humility, his Evangelical poverty, his disengagement from all affection to earthly things, his spirit of penance, his modest comportment, his love of prayer, and his care to avoid every thing which might make him lose sight of the presence of God.

Benedict having one day asked of M. Mancini, administrator of the House called the Hospitium Evangelicum leave to set out on his Pilgrimage to Loretto; this gentleman thought it would be a satisfaction to him to recommend for a companion for his journey, a poor man belonging to the same house, who was a man of a virtuous and edifying life. But the Servant of God begged to be excused from accepting the proposed companion: alledging as a reason of his refusal, his fear that the company of another Pilgrim, how good a man soever he might be in himself, might be to him an occasion of some hinderance or distraction, and withdraw him from that inward recollection, and uninterupted prayer, which he always practised all the time he was travelling.

Mr. Zaccarelli his friend and benefactor having offered him some money for his expences in his journey to Loretto,

Benedict

Benedict refused to accept any part of it, alledging as his reason, that he had in his possession a piece of money of the value of ten sous, or five pence English : and that this sum was sufficient for him at present. Animated by the same spirit of Evangelical poverty, he at first refused a pair of shoes which the same M. Zaccarelli offered him. But this gentleman pressing him to accept them, at the same time shewed him three other pair of shoes which had been used : Benedict therefore at length yielded to the solicitations of his Benefactor and accepted a pair, but chose those which had been most worn.

As he used to wear a straw hat, which was all unsewed and torn, they had all imaginable difficulty, to prevail upon him to accept another which was a little better, though that itself was very old and in a bad condition.

From the enquiries that have been made, and the informations that have been given at Loretto, we learn some other particulars of his conduct, which are no less edifying than those which have been already mentioned.

M. Verdelli, Clerk of the Chapel in that famous Church of Loretto, and whose business it is to superintend the Lamps that are kept constantly lighted, deposes, that he was penetrated with admiration, when he beheld the respectful countenance of
this

this Pilgrim, his continual prayer, and the profound humility with which he presented himself in the presence of God in his Temple.

Mr. Valeri, the Sacristan gives the same testimony, and moreover adds, that at the usual hour of dinner, when all the rest of the people went out of the Church, Benedict, regardless of his corporal wants, went and placed himself in a corner of the Church, where he thought he might not be perceived; and there, with a countenance enflamed by devotion, he saw him smite his breast, and by other exteriour actions give vent and scope to the pious motions of his soul.

The same Ecclesiastick having remarked the extreme endeavours of the Servant of God to conceal every thing which might give any one a good opinion of him: went and shut himself up in a Confessional to watch him at ease through the latices, and to see him exercise the repeated acts of his fervent devotion.

All the time that this pious Pilgrim remained at Loretto, he not only did not ask any alms, but even refused what was voluntarily offered to him: if it exceeded what was necessary for his immediate relief.

Messrs. Verdelli and Valeri having entertained the greatest esteem for his virtues, looked out for a lodging for him in Loretto, in order to fave him the trouble of going every night to a Barn, at a great diftance, where he ordinarily took up his lodging, and every morning returned again to the Church. Having found one, in the houfe of Mr. Sori, they conducted him to it. Benedict accepted their kindnefs with gratitude. But as they had prepared a room for him with a bed in it, he thought this lodging was too fumptuous for a poor man, like him. They then offered him another, cut out of the Rock, under the ftreet: this he looked on as more fuitable to his condition, and accepted it.

Mr. Sori, fometimes offered him fome victuals from his table, but he conftantly begged to be excufed from accepting it. A Poor man, faid he, ought not to eat fuch kinds of food as are prepared for the Rich: but he ought to be content with what is left at their table. In like manner, whenever any one offered him a whole loaf of bread, he would never take it; thinking himfelf unworthy of eating any thing but fcraps. He entertained the fame fcruple againft all other kinds of food: and in effect never eat any thing but fcraps.

CHAP.

CHAP. XIV.

The manner in which the Servant of God lived at Rome, after he had fixed his Residence in that City.

BENEDICT, who from his youth had had the happiness to understand the meaning of these words of our Saviour, *Blessed are the Poor in Spirit*, carried his observance of them to a very eminent degree of perfection. For it may be truly said, that he practised the humility and poverty recommended in the Gospel, in the utmost rigour. This was evidently his particular vocation: and that kind of sanctity which he embraced, was the most convincing proof of his faithfully corresponding to that vocation.

Some accounts of the life which he led at Rome, from the time he made that the place of his fixed residence, furnish us with a multitude of proofs of this faithful correspondence with his vocation: and at the same time are capable of affording us great instruction and edification.

There is in the quarter of the Amphitheatre of Flavian, otherwise called the Colifeo, near the Street of the Cross, some ancient ruins, and a great extent of walls, half demolished. Having found in these ruins, a hole of a sufficient depth to hold

him

him and fhelter him in a tolerable degree
from the weather; he immediately thought
he could be contented with this place for
his habitation. And indeed he had no o-
ther for feveral years. Thither therefore
he retired every night to take his reft.
And being refolved to carry his Crofs after
his Divine Redeemer, and to imitate his
poverty who had no poffeffions nor *place
where to lay his head*: Benedict thought
himfelf highly happy that Providence had
prepared a place for him where he might
pafs the nights in peace and contented
tranquility, and be fheltered from the in-
clemency of the feafons, and the nocturnal
dews.

The life of this poor follower of Jefus
Chrift, was the fame as it had been for a
long time in every place where he had been:
that is, a life of <u>continual prayer</u>. Having (91, 97)
employed the whole day in this holy occu- (89)
pation, he thought the time ftill too fhort. (100)
Wherefore after having paffed the day
fometimes in one Church, and fometimes
in another, <u>praying moft commonly upon
his knees, and at other times ftanding, and
always keeping his body</u> as ftill as if he
was a ftatue: he employed alfo a part of
the night in this holy exercife. If at any
time he quitted the Churches, it was for
the purpofe of going to the Colifeo to be
prefent at the Inftructions which are called
the *Evangelical Inftructions*, at which he
failed

failed not to be prefent every day in the year.

A kind of life fo hard and auftere, joined with his cuftom of praying on his knees the greateft part of the day, failed not foon to weaken him, and impair his health: and brought on a swelling in his knees, which increafing by degrees, in the year 1780 threatned him with a fpeedy death.

A poor beggar named Theodore, who alfo had the reputation of being a very virtuous and thoroughly good Chriftian, perceiving his fituation, took pity on him, and perfuaded him to go with him to Mr. Paul Mancini, who was the Director and Adminiftrator of the Evangelical Hofpitium, to whom he prefented him as an object truly deferving of his charitable care and protection.

M. Mancini immediately took the Servant of God under his care, and put him into his Alms-houfe, which was eftablifhed for the reception of twelve poor men.

By taking the medicines proper for his diforder, and a more fubftantial food, he foon grew well. And now finding himfelf out of danger, and his health re-eftablifhed; he made all hafte to go and feek his Benefactor: to whom he faid, " You fee " me, Sir, now perfectly cured: this cha-" rity, which you have done to me in tak-" ing care of me in your Alms-houfe, you
" may

" may now exercise in favour of some
" other poor person who is in greater
" need than I am at present. I now find
" myself in a condition of going to seek
" my support at the door of some Convent.
" But by what means can I be able to ac-
" knowledge in a proper manner my sen-
" timents of gratitude for your goodness,
" and make you a suitable recompence!
" I do not in the least doubt but my
" swelling would have speedily brought
" me to my grave. It is therefore owing
" to your goodness that I am now alive.
" ———It is God (said M. Mancini) to
" whom you ought to return your thanks.
" It is he who has restored you to your
" health. I beg you will be so charitable
" as to recommend me to God in your
" prayers, and I shall be very much
" obliged to you. Ah, Sir, said Benedict,
" that I will do with all my heart; and
" will continue so to do all the days of my
" life."

The care which the Abbe Mancini had
rendered to the Servant of God during
his illness, had enabled him to discover in
him a degree of virtue far beyond what is
common, and such extraordinary sentiments of Religion which all his humility
was not able to conceal. This made him
entertain such an high opinion of him : that
contrary to the Custom and the Rule which
he had made for that House of not retain-
ing

ing therein the poor which he admitted but only for a certain time, or as long as their neceſſity ſhould require; he continued to admit him to come and lay in the Houſe every night, which favour the Servant of God continued to receive till the year 1783, which was the year of his death.

It is proper here to give an account of two particular occurrences of his life which happened during his journeys to Loretto, and which ſhew how little account he made of himſelf. M. Mancini from whom we learn theſe particulars, kept a literary correſpondence with a Nun of the Monaſtery of St. Clare at Montelupone in the Dioceſs of Loretto. He therefore being deſirous of embracing the opportunity of Benedict's journey to that place, ſent a letter to her by his hand, in which among many other edifying things, he ſaid, *My letter will be delivered to you by a Saint who ſpends his whole life in prayer.* Benedict executed his commiſſion, and delivered the letter to the Nun, with whom he ſpent ſome little time in pious converſation, which concluded by a mutual promiſe of praying for each other for the future.

The Nun then read the letter, and having ſhewn it to the other Nuns, the whole Community immediately came to recommend themſelves to the prayers of the man who had been declared to be a Saint.

K   Benedict,

Benedict, by this assemblage and request of the whole Community was thrown into such a state of confusion, as scarce to know what they said to him: and without waiting for an answer to the Letter he had brought, he presently moved from off the premises, and went out of the Monastery, into which he never after entered so long as he lived.

When Benedict had returned to Rome, M. Mancini asked him for the answer to the letter which he had sent by him to the Nun. Benedict replied, "I received no "answer from her." And then in a few words he gave him an account of what had passed. M. Mancini then perceived how great was his humility: and from that time entertained a still greater opinion of his sanctity.

In the following year M. Mancini sent by him a letter to a Nun of the Convent of S. Clare at Montechio: but in this he took greater precaution than he had done before. He mentioned the opinion he entertained concerning Benedict, but he recommended to her above all things to take particular care that neither she, nor any one of the Community, should shew to the Servant of God any particular mark of esteem or regard.

This letter was delivered with the same exactness as the former had been. The Nun communicated the contents of it to her

her companions. And they were no less desirous of seeing and entertaining this pious Pilgrim, than the Nuns of Montelupone: but being previously admonished, they acted more prudently. They came to see him separately, one after another: and in order to engage him to continue a longer time in their House, that every one might have the satisfaction of seeing him without giving him any occasion of suspecting their intention; they ordered something to be brought for him to eat. By this means every one of them was pleased and edified. They wanted likewise to furnish him with some provision for the rest of his journey: and accordingly offered him several things: but he refused to accept of any thing that was offered to him: being fully resolved to adhere to and observe the rule he had prescribed to himself, of *taking no thought for the morrow.*

This time he waited for an answer to M. Mancini's letter, which he promised to deliver to him. The Nun gave him an account of what had passed, and in particular of their circumspection: but at the same time she did not forget to make M. Mancini pay for that circumspection, by earnestly begging that he himself would recommend that Community to the prayers of that good man: and in particular

that

that he would pray for them at the time when he should go to Communion.

‘ While Mr. Mancini was speaking to Benedict upon this subject, he perceived the uneasiness which such a request gave to this poor disciple of Jesus Christ, inasmuch as it indicated that they made some account of his prayers: so that he had no other answer than this to give to their request. "Henceforward I wish not to have "any correspondence with Nuns. For "who am I that I should be able to afford "them benefit by my Prayers, and my "Communions.

Doubtless it will also afford satisfaction to the reader to see the Account which Mr. Mancini himself gives of the conduct of this Servant of God, all the time that he resided in his Hospitium.

This then is the testimony which Mr. Mancini gave of him immediately after his death. And it is an additional proof of what we have said, that he was almost every moment of his time employed in prayer, and made it his continual occupation.

The servant of God was always very careful to return to the Hospitium at a proper hour. If he arrived before it was opened; in that case, while the others entered into conversation when they were assembled about the door waiting for the Guardian, he commonly went and placed

himself

himself behind a little column which made
a part of the front of the house of the Che-
valier Santarelli, which was just by. There
he remained all the while upon his knees
in prayer, till the time that he heard the
door open. Then, going in with the o-
ther poor men, he stopped in the first
room where the bed was, that was prepared
for him: while the others went on and
continued their conversation in an inner
room where there were ten other beds.
All the Poor being arrived, and the Guardian calling them to prayers, Benedict went
in, and assisted at them with such recollection and devotion, that all the others were
highly edified by his behaviour.

- Prayers being ended he returned to his
apartment, and then began his private prayers, which he continued to say even after
all the lights were put out: so that no one
ever saw him pull of his cloaths to go to
bed. He also arose in the night to say his
prayers: and made a great number of ejaculatory prayers. And the good man
Theodore, who was then Guardian of the
Hospitium, and who lay near to his apartment, frequently heard him, during the
night, say, *Lord have mercy on me; my
God have mercy on me.* The other poor men
also frequently heard him, repeat the same
expressions.

- Benedict entertained a great regard for
this Hospitium, because no poor persons

were

were admitted into it, but those who lived the life of good Christians, and in which no disagreements, contentions, or unbecoming words were ever tolerated.

In the morning he arose before the hour prescribed, and employed himself in private prayer, or in meditation, till the time that all the Community were called to prayers: at which he never failed to be present with the other poor men.

After this he went out of the Hospitium; and he was always observed to go alone, and saying his prayers, towards some Church: and he generally went to that of S. Mary di Monti, as it is commonly called, where he continued upon his knees in prayer till about noon. Sometimes he divided the morning in such a manner, as to pass one half of it in one Church, and the other half in another Church.

At noon he went to the door of some Convent to beg one of the portions which are every day distributed to the poor. And then going to that Church where the Laus-perenne or forty hours prayer was held, and consequently where the Blessed Sacrament was exposed, he there passed the rest of the day.

Before he eat the small quantity which he took for his dinner, he seemed for some time entirely absorpt in God. The Guardian of the House of charity of S. Pantaleon in the Mountain, says he observed
that

that every time he came to receive the portion and the bread which they diſtributed to the poor: before this Servant of God would taſte any thing, he always took the veſſel which contained his food in both his hands, and held it up towards heaven as offering it to God, praying at the ſame time for the ſpace of five or ſix minutes, with a kind of extatic fervour, while the other poor had began to eat what was given to them.

Theſe accounts ſuffice to prove, that his life was a life of continual prayer. Every day he ſaid the Divine Office: and the time which was not employed in reading books of piety, he ſpent either in meditation on the ſufferings of our Divine Redeemer, or elſe in ſaying a great number of vocal prayers, or pious ejaculations.

M. Mancini here relates nothing but what he was an eye-witneſs of, or which are publicly known. The plain ſtile in which he writes his account, ſhews him to be a faithful Hiſtorian. He uſes neither eulogiums, nor reflections. Let us then imitate this prudent reſervedneſs, and confine ourſelves to aſſemble together into one picture the outlines of the conſtant, uniform, and hidden life of the Servant of God during the time that he lived at Rome.

In the firſt place therefore he lived a life of perpetual and inviolable ſilence: never

ſpeaking

speaking but of God ; and holding no conversation with men. In the space of a whole month scarce could any one hear him speak so much as even a few words. Whenever he did speak, his answers were comprised in a very few words: for he was always careful never to dispense with his law of silence, but only when humility or charity required him to speak.

Secondly, he led a life of retirement and solitude : having no one for his companion but God, nor did he keep any company but with God. He avoided all communication with men, all the tumult of publick places, the dissipation of walks, the sight of amusements so common at Rome : living as if he was in the very midst of a desert, although he was in the midst of a City inhabited by a great number of strangers, and which presents to the sight a most busy, changing, and variegated scene.

Thirdly, he led a life of the greatest self-denial : being destitute of every thing ; disengaged from every earthly affection ; and unnoticed by all mankind : he desired no other riches than those of Evangelical poverty : no other pleasures than the exercises of penance and mortification, and no other marks of distinction, than that of being the object of universal contempt.

Fourthly, he led a life of the most rigorous

rous poverty* : he received no fuccour of
affiftance from his family, to whom even
his very exiftence was unknown : he afked
nothing of any body, but only received
with humility what was voluntarily offered
to him ; and with a generous charity dif-
tributed to the other poor all that was not
neceffary for the relief of his immediate
wants : he was expofed to the viciffitudes
and inclemencies of the weather : without
fhelter againft the colds of winter, or the
heats of fummer : and having nothing
more than other ordinary poor : very old
garments, very coarfe food, and for the
three firft years, no other lodging but a
hole in the ruins of an old wall.

Fifthly, he led a life of the moft auftere
penance : for to this extreme poverty and
privation of all earthly goods ; he joined
an almoft continual abftinence, and frequent fafts, though his conftitution was
weakened and rendered feeble : to thefe
alfo he added nightly vigils, and other
particular mortifications. And notwithftanding

* All his moveables confifted in a little bafket,
wherein he ufed to keep his Breviary, and fome
other books of devotion, and a wooden bowl in
which he received his broth at the gates of the
Monafteries. A piece of it is broken off at the
edge, fo that it could not be filled ; and as it
had been fplit through the middle, he had got it
cramped with three pieces of iron-wire.

standing his habitual infirmities, he perfe-
vered in the practice of a kind of penance
which frequently occasioned the most lively and insupportable pains; and that was
by his ordinarily praying on his knees,
which laid him under the necessity of resting the whole weight of his body on two
painful tumours, which covered both his
knees.

Sixthly, he embraced with a cordial affection, all the humiliations which accompany a life of poverty and penance. His
humility made him look on himself as one
of the greatest of sinners. It was for this
reason, and to make some kind of atone-
ment for his sins, that he chose to lead a
life of reproach and contempt: this was
his motive for undertaking all the austerities of that extraordinary penance which
he continued to practise till his death: this
was the reason why he hid himself among
the multitude of poor beggars: why he
chose to be looked on as the outcast of the
world: why he chose to cover himself with
rags and tatters, instead of garments: why
he chose to place a barrier of disgust between himself and the rest of mankind, and
disfigured the lineaments of a face naturally amiable and attractive, under an abject
and forbidding appearance: and in a word
this was the reason why through a love of
penance and ignominy, he abandoned to
the bites of disagreeable insects, that
humbled

humbled body which God now glorifies, and at this prefent time preferves from corruption, and from being the food of worms.

Such was the exteriour and publick life of Benedict during all the years he lived at Rome: a kind of life which he embraced voluntarily, and of his own free choice. For this kind of life, he quitted his country, and his parents, and relinquifhed a decent patrimony, and all the profpect he had of being fettled in an eafy and happy ftation in life. This is undoubtedly an extraordinary kind of life; and though it is not propofed to us for our imitation; yet it ought to ferve as a fpur and encouragement to our zeal in the fervice of God, and incline us to fhake off that floth, that delicacy and felf-love, which we have contracted by being engaged in the ftation in which Providence has placed us.

The humility, the poverty, and mortifications of the Crofs, always appear to be folly in the eyes of thofe who are worldly-wife. But perhaps the penitential life of Benedict would not appear fo extraordinary to us, if we did not live in an age of fuch general corruption and diffolution of morals, which hinders us from knowing and confining ourfelves within the bounds of what is really neceffary, and inclines us

to

to follow with eagernefs all the pleafures and vanities of the age.

Let us therefore cautioufly guard againft that precipitate pride, which frequently cenfures what it is ignorant of, and condemns what it does not underftand: and before we pronounce our fentence concerning this good man, let us read with attention the lives of S. Paul the firft Hermit, of S. Anthony, S. Mary of Egypt, S. Simeon the Stylite, and of many others in the primitive Church who have been a kind of Martyrs of Chriftian penance.

As members of the Church of Chrift we ought at leaft to look with refpect upon the life of this holy man, and wait for the event of the folemn examination of a multitude of wonders, which fame has publifhed as being wrought by God at his interceffion, and by his means. And which by the prudent circumfpection of thofe to whom this tafk is committed, will be fo nicely examined, that even the very enemies of our holy Faith, will find themfelves under a neceffity of acknowledgeing the juftnefs of the Sentence they will pronounce.

CHAP.

CHAP. XV.

Gives an account of the laft year of the life of the Servant of God.

THE Secrets of Kings ought to be inviolably kept, but it is a duty incumbent on us to publifh to the world the wonders which God has wrought in favour of his Elect.

Divine Providence having ordained that during the laft year of the life of Benedict Jofeph Labre, I fhould be the depofitary of the moft fecret thoughts of his Soul: I look upon myfelf obliged to publifh all that the knowledge of which may contribute to the glory of God, to the honour of his Servant, and to the edification of the Faithful.

In the month of June 1782, juft after I had celebrated Mafs in the Church of St. Ignatius belonging to the Roman College: I perceived a man whofe appearance at firft fight was difagreeable and forbidding, his legs were half naked, his cloaths were tied round the waift with an old cord: his head uncombed; he was badly cloathed and wrapt up in an old and ragged coat: and in his outward appearance he feemed to be the moft miferable beggar that I had ever feen. Such was the appearance of Benedict the firft time I beheld him.

When I had finished my thanksgiving after Mass, he came up to me, and with a great deal of modesty and respect told me that he had prepared himself to make a General Confession, and begged that I would be so charitable as to hear it, and to appoint a day for that purpose: he assured me that I might rely on his sincerity: because he did not come with any intention of imposing upon me: and had nothing in view but the sanctification of his Soul.

These few plain words, and the manner in which he uttered them, immediately insinuated themselves into my heart, and engaged my affection for him. I therefore granted his request, and made no doubt but that he was a good man, and well disposed.

According to my promise I met him at the time we had agreed on. The Servant of God began with order and regularity to lay open the state of his whole life, and even to explain the minutest particulars with the nicest exactness: from the time of his infancy to the present day; and even mentioned some things which were not to happen to him till after his death. He discovered to me both the present state of his Soul, and the honours which God had in store for him; with the same clearness and precision, with which (in several subsequent conversations I had with him)

he discovered to me many future events
which had been revealed to him.

I soon perceived in the soul of Benedict
an extraordinary light, which immediately
threw me into surprize and astonishment.
By the manner in which he gave me an
account of the whole state of his Soul, I
perceived that he had a profound knowledge of the whole law of God. He spoke
with a wonderful order and clearness on
the concatenation of revealed truths and
the connection of every virtue; the relation they have to the law of God, and to
each other: and he explained the distinc-
tive marks or characters of each particular
virtue, and the different degrees of perfection which they contain.

At this my astonishment redoubled: I
could not persuade myself, that a man, who
had never studied, could be able to speak
on the most sublime subjects in the same
manner as if he had been one of the most
learned Professors of Divinity. I therefore interrupted him, to ask him if he had
studied Divinity? " I, Father, replied he
" with a great deal of humility; No, I ne-
" ver studied Divinity; I am but a poor
" ignorant man." This answer threw me
again into all my doubts; so that I could
not determine whether the knowledge
which he had, was the effect of study and
his own reflections: or whether God had

not

not imparted it to him by immediate communication and infpiration.

The clearnefs and exactnefs with which Benedict expreffed all his thoughts, unfolded all the motions of his heart, and rendered them in a manner vifible to my eyes: the particular account of the afflicting trials through which God had made him pafs, the graces and favours which he had received from God, and what he had always done to correfpond with thefe favours and graces: the tendernefs of his confcience; his fingular purity of heart; his fentiments of profound humility; and his fimplicity like that of an infant, joined with an extraordinary prudence, all being united and carried to a very eminent degree, immediately fixed my ideas and judgment concerning him. I faw in this poor beggar, an extraordinary man, whom God, by ways which confound all human prudence, made ufe of as an inftrument of his great defigns. I perceived myfelf excited to enter into the views of his divine Providence, and I thought myfelf obliged to make a fuitable return for the confidence which Benedict repofed in me: and to render him all the fervice which might be in my power.

The more I became acquainted with his confcience, fo much the more I admired his noble and exalted Soul, and the extraordinary graces and favours with which he was

was enriched. God has fometimes difcovered to him the ftate of my own Soul,
and my moft fecret thoughts: and Benedict has many times mentioned them to
me. Without doubt Providence had fo
ordained: that the Revelation made to
Benedict concerning the ftate of my own
intetiour, might be a certain affurance of
the predictions which related to himfelf,
and which were fucceffively to happen to
him till the end of his life.

I ought here to add, that in every converfation I had with him, he always acquainted me with fomething that God had
operated in his Soul, and that thefe things
in a great meafure related to the manner
in which he would be pleafed to render
him glorious in this world, immediately after his death.

We have feen that the Servant of God,
from his infancy to the end of his life, advanced progreffively and by large fteps, in
the obfervance of all the laws and commandments of God. But it may truly be
faid that in the laft year of his life, he led
upon earth the life of an Angel: by an ad-
dition of fervour which is impoffible to be
expreffed. He poured out his foul with
the utmoft humility in the prefence of the
Lord; his thoughts and his heart were entirely abforpt in the love of God; and his
body which was mortified and brought into

                                          perfect

perfect fubjection appeared to be no more than a fkeleton, covered only with a fkin.

On Friday in Paffion-week, which was five days before his death, I had a converfation with him, and which was the laft time I ever fpoke to him : and this converfation feems to be of fo much importance, that I think it is very neceffary to give a particular account of it.

It is well known that this day is fet apart by the Church for the folemn annual Commemoration of the forrows of the Bleffed Virgin. On the morning of this day he came to the Church of the Roman College, to make his Confeffion. I found him near the altar of the Bleffed Virgin, employed in profound recollection and meditation : and his body was in that ftate of immobility, to which he was accuftomed when he prayed. I looked at him with a great deal of attention, and was furprifed to fee, that, contrary to his cuftom, he had a ftick in his hand. This was now become neceffary to fupport his emaciated and weakened body. See there, faid I within myfelf, and while I was fpeaking to him, fee to what a condition his aufterities have reduced him ; it will not be long before he dies a martyr of penance. And all the while, notwithftanding the particular regard I had for him, and which he perfectly well knew, in confequence of all that I had faid to him concerning the feverities which
he

he exercised upon his body; it never once came into my mind to speak to him about his health: much less did it come into my mind to exhort him to take care of himself, and to moderate his penitential austerities.

I continued to speak to him, and at the same time looked at and reflected on his tattered garments, which appeared so disagreeable to the fight; his flesh of a livid and mortified appearance: and I particularly took notice of his right hand and arm: when immediately some thoughts, very unlike the former, arose in a confused manner in my mind. Perhaps, said I to myself, these rags which seem now so disagreeable, may in a short time be preferred to the richest silks: perhaps they may be honoured as the relicks of a Saint: but, thought I but before these rags can come to the point of veneration, very great and extraordinary events must happen. Oh how great consolation did it afford me! How much reason have I to bless God who is the author of all Sanctity, and who is so wonderful in all his Saints; to be, as I was, immediately after his death, a witness of the eagerness of all the inhabitants of Rome, great and small, from the common people to those of the highest Rank; to fee and venerate those very rags, and every thing else which had belonged to the Servant of God.

In

In fine I muſt add, what indeed muſt appear very extraordinary, that neither at this, nor at any other time, did it come into my mind to exhort the Servant of God not to be ſo careleſs concerning the outward appearance of his body, nor even to free himſelf from the bites of the troubleſome inſects. that were about him: and which could not fail of being to him the occaſion of a torment in its own nature as humiliating as it was inſupportable.

It was for this laſt reaſon that I always took the precaution never to hear his confeſſion, but in a Confeſſional, on purpoſe that there might be ſome kind of ſeparation between us: but for this time I changed my opinion concerning that practice; and thought it was more juſt for me to take ſuch a precaution in favour of the perſons who frequented the ſame Confeſſional, than it was for me to take that precaution in favour of myſelf alone.

I therefore led him to the gate of the Roman College, and made him go into the Porter's room without any body's perceiving him: there I ſat myſelf down to hear him: and he being upon his knees, two floods of tears ſtreamed from his eyes: but though his tears ran in abundance, they were not accompanied with any ſighs or groans. The Servant of God then repeated to me many things which particu-

larly

larly related to me, and which he had told
me at different times before.

I obferved that he at this time fhewed a
greater earneftnefs to make his Confeffion
than I had ever remarked before: but at
the fame time I found not the leaft thing,
that was, properly fpeaking, matter of Confeffion. Peace, tranquility, and confola-
tions, overflowed his Soul, which from the
time of his laft Confeffion had been entirely free from all temptation, and from all interiour anguifh. This was without doubt
owing entirely to the goodnefs of Almighty
God, who having made him pafs through a
great number of fevere trials, had brought
him to this ferene and cloudlefs day which
fixes the juft man in the ftate of perfection,
and makes the dawn of an approaching
happy eternity fhine upon his Soul. I
ought indeed at that time, to have made
this reflection: but God, who was pleafed
that the defigns of his Providence fhould
remain hidden till the end of the life of
his Servant, did not permit me to perceive,
that Benedict was then come to prepare
himfelf to take his flight to the eternal
manfions of the Saints.

A new circumftance which then happened might alfo have given me fome
forefight of his death. At other times,
before we parted, it was always our cuftom to agree upon a day when he fhould
come again: I was going to afk the que-
ftion,

paired, and that he funk by degrees under the austerities of penance.

The fatigues of long journeys had exhausted his health and strength. He had experienced and gone through the change of different climates, the vicissitude of seasons; he had endured very severe colds, and excessive heats; and had travelled to places at an immense distance from each other; so that his zeal seemed to know no bounds, nor was it to be overcome by any obstacles whatever. This was in the first years of his penitential life: but after this he embraced a course of penance of a kind quite contrary to the former. He gave himself up to a sedentary life, to a total cessation of exercise, and to continual prayer. He never went out of one Church, but to go into another: where he remained either kneeling, or standing almost all the day, as still and unmoved as a statue: such was the life of Benedict from the day when he fixed his residence at Rome. Nor could his health suffer less from that extraordinary kind of torment, of which we spoke before, which he endured by kneeling always upon his swelled knees: which deprived him of ease by day, and of sleep by night, and moreover in the latter end of his days his body was covered with sores and ulcers.

To these sufferings which he endured with the most consummate patience, he

added

added fasts and abstinence to a most rigorous degree. His whole sustenance consisted in a small portion which he went to receive at the gate of some Convent or other house of publick Charity; but he did not go every day to receive even this. And amongst the scraps that were distributed to the poor, he frequently and by way of preference chose those which were the worst, and least capable of nourishing his body. It is very true that latterly, with regard to his food I endeavoured to moderate his indefatigable inclination to mortification, and ordered that amongst the different things that were offered to him, he should not choose that which he thought to be the worst; but so trifling a mitigation as this, was not sufficient, to prevent the consequences of his penitential austerities.

The commencement of Lent was to Benedict another motive of redoubling these austerities. He observed the fast, and abstinence still more rigourously than he had done in the foregoing years: and at this time he would not allow himself any mitigation, by making use of the general dispensation granted by the Pope. And it was only at the near approach of death, when he found his strength exhausted, that he yielded to the representations of some compassionate Christian, and consented to eat some hard eggs, and to mix a little vinegar with the water which he drank.

M A body

A body treated with such severity could not fail of falling a speedy victim of penance: and the lively affection of his heart at the same time contributed to hasten the consummation of his sacrifice.

None but truly generous Christians can conceive how great is the affliction of a Soul which burns with an ardent love of God and its neighbour: when on the one hand it sees the most heinous outrages offered to the Sovereign Majesty of God, and on the other hand sees senseless mortals committing these outrages, running headlong to their own destruction, and plunging themselves into the most dreadful and irremediable evils.

Benedict entertained in his heart a most ardent love of God: and his love for his neighbour was exceeded by nothing but by the love which he entertained for God. He saw the goodness of God despised, and his very blessings bestowed on man made use of as means and instruments of offending him: he saw Religion rent in pieces by Heresies and Schisms: attacked by infidels, disgraced by the vices and scandalous lives of Catholicks; its Sacraments and its Temples profaned, and the sacred institutions of Penance, the Fasts and Abstinences prescribed by the Church publickly transgressed. Benedict continually loved all mankind whom he considered as *his fellow creatures,* created like himself according to

God's

God's own likeness, and intended to partake of his divine blessings; *as Christians*, like him redeemed by the precious blood of Jesus Christ; and *as brethren* whom God had commanded him to love, and for whose Salvation God always inspired him with a most lively and ardent zeal; and it was this love of God and his neighbour, jointly considered with the injuries that were offered to God by infidels, and scandalous sinners, and the foresight of the eternal perdition into which such sinners were plunging their own souls; that cut him to the heart, and filled his soul with the most lively and compassionate regret. Those who knew the heart of the Servant of God, attest, that to make some kind of compensation to God for these injuries offered to him, and obtain mercy, and the grace of a sincere repentance for the offenders; was the motive of his continual fasts, his penitential austerities, his passing the nights in watching and prayer, his undertaking so many journeys of devotion with so much courage and resolution, and executing them though they cost him so much labour and fatigue.

Thus it was that his love of God, and of his neighbour, made him suffer a kind of double martyrdom during his whole life, and at length carried him out of the world in the flower of his age.

Wednesday in Holy-week of the year 1783, was the time which God had fixed

to

to put an end, both to his penitential auſterities, and to his mortal life. He ſeemed to have entertained a particular affection for the Church of S. Mary di Monti. For, for the ſpace of about eight years during which he fixed his reſidence at Rome, he commonly went thither at the uſual hour of opening its doors, and there he remained occupied in aſſiſting at the Maſſes that were celebrated, in ſaying his prayers, or in hearing the word of God, till the Divine Offices were all finiſhed.

On this day after having employed the whole morning in theſe holy exerciſes, about one o'clock in the afternoon, he was ſeen to fall down on one of the ſteps, leading to the door of that Church : the ſpectators immediately ran to aſſiſt him : he begged they would give him a glaſs of water, which was preſently brought to him: he took it in his hands, and with ardent ſighs and eyes lifted up to Heaven he devoutly offered it up to God. It was remarked that after he had drank, he again lifted up his ſwooning eyes, and joining his hands, he returned thanks to God for this ſmall relief, with a devotion which penetrated the hearts of all thoſe that were about him and moved them to have compaſſion on him.

Mr. Charles Anthony Maria Rinaldi, who was one of the eye-witneſſes of this tranſaction, and from whom I heard it, related

lated it to me with a heart still glowing with compassion, and with tears standing in his eyes. The Servant of God found himself so weak that he was not able to get up, nor to stand when he was lifted up. Some offered to carry him to the Hospital that was hard by: others offered him their house, and with a great deal of tenderness desired he would let them carry him thither. He kindly thanked them for their charitable care of him, but excused himself from giving them any further trouble. At that instant Mr. Francis Zaccarelli arrived, who lives just by the Barracks of the Corsican Guards, near the Church of St. Mary di Monti, and seeing him in this condition, he said to him: *Benedict, you are not well: it is necessary to take care of ourselves : will you let me conduct you to my house? To your house; said* Benedict, *Yes, I accept your kind offer.* Mr Zaccarelli who is a Butcher, well known for his good religious life, and his particular affection for Benedict, accordingly procured some people to carry him to his house, and to lay him down upon a bed, with all his cloaths on.

They then were under no uneasiness on account of this accident, as they imagined it was only the effect of an excessive abstinence, and that when he should have taken some nourishment, he would recover his strength again; and accordingly they gave it to him in abundance. But by reason of his

extreme

extreme weaknefs, this very nourifhment, inftead of being beneficial, was pernicious to him: and his fwoonings fenfibly increafed. It was then thought proper to give him fome bifcuit dipt in wine, in order to revive his opprefled fpirits: but now he was not able to fwallow any thing. The Rev. Fr. Pecillo one of the Directors of the Society of pious Labourers, was then prefent, and was the perfon who had fuggefted the giving him the bifcuit dipt in wine. He immediately perceived the dangerous flate he was in, and afked him if any confiderable time had paffed, fince he had been at the Sacraments: and if he was confcious of any thing that might make him uneafy in his mind? He replied that it was but a little time fince he had been at the Sacraments; that he thanked God, he knew not of any thing to make him uneafy; and that his foul was in peace. We have already mentioned that he communicated on the Friday before, in the Church of St. Ignatius, from the hands of M. Balducci; on Palm Sunday he alfo had communicated in the Church of S. Mary Major, which is a fact we have been informed of by Mr. Mancini: and although we have no abfolute certainty of it, yet there is all reafon to believe that he had the happinefs to receive the B. Sacrament, on this fame Wednefday morning in the Church of St. Mary di Monti.

In the mean while the Servant of God was approaching to his laſt hour: he had loſt his ſpeech and almoſt loſt his ſenſes. They ran to give an account of his ſituation to the Rector of the Pariſh of S. Saviour di Monti who at that time was alſo ill, and therefore ſent his Vicar to attend the ſick man. But as Benedict was not able to give any ſign of being in his ſenſes, at any of the four viſits which the Vicar made to him : it was not poſſible to adminiſter the Viaticum to him : and therefore he contented himſelf with giving him Extreme Unction.

The Fathers of the Congregation of Jeſus of Nazareth who are diſtinguiſhed by their Charity for people in their agony, being informed of the ſituation of Benedict, went one after another to aſſiſt and continue with him for that purpoſe till his dying moment. The Rev. F. Anthony Tapies, Superior of that Order, was at ſupper when the news was brought to him; he immedittely quitted the table and made all poſſible haſte to the dying man. He was afterward relieved by F. Angelo Pelutoſe: after whom came F. Andrew, Adami, who was preſent with him when he breathed his laſt.

The perſons who ſurrounded his bed were deſirous to invoke the Interceſſion and Protection of the bleſſed Virgin in his favour; and for that purpoſe all kneeled

down

down to fay the Litany of Loretto. And at thefe words, *Holy Mary, pray for him,* this good man, who had always entertained a particular Veneration for and Devotion to the bleffed Mother of God, without any convulfion or fenfible agony, calmly refigned his Soul into the hands of his Creator, in the beginning of the evening of Wednefday the 16th of April 1783, being then thirty five years and twenty one days old.

His departure out of this life happened at the very moment when all the Clocks in Rome began to announce the time of faying the Salve Regina, which is a Form of Prayer appointed by the Chief Paftor of the Church, to implore the interceffion and protection of the Bleffed Virgin, for the preffing neceffities of the Church.

CHAP. XVII.

Relates the extraordinary things which happened either before or immediately after the death of the Servant of God.

IT ordinarily happens that all that relates to this world is over with a man when he is once laid in the grave. That is the fatal period both of his frame, and of his hopes. But on the contrary the memory of the Saints is immortal. It is when they are arrived at their Tomb, that their glory commences:

commences: and the hasty succession of ages produces no other effect with regard to them; but that of increasing their fame.

This is one of the means by which the Divine Oracles are fulfilled. He who has renounced every thing in this world in order to carry the Cross after Jesus Christ, sometimes receives even in this life an hundred fold reward, for all that he had renounced. We have seen that Benedict had renounced every thing, in order to bury himself in a life of poverty, humility, and obscurity: and it seems that God has now thought proper to make the honours which will be rendered to his memory, bear a proportion to the humiliations which he practised in his life.

Fifteen days before the death of Benedict, a Nun who is remarkable for her piety, and who at the times when the Servant of God made his Pilgrimages to Loretto, had some conversations with him upon subjects of piety, was informed by God, that he would shortly crop a beatiful flower in the garden of M. Paul Mancini. By this garden she understood the Hospital of the Poor, of which he has the care and administration. The letter which she sent to that Reverend Ecclesiastick; was sent before any one could suspect that the death of this poor Servant of God was so near. At the time of his death, the same Nun wrote again and acquainted him that the flower which

which she had mentioned before, was Benedict Joseph Labre, whom the Lord had then transplanted into the happy Gardens of the heavenly Jerusalem.

At the same time God gave a similar notice of his death at Loretto. Benedict, during the days which he remained at Loretto, in his annual Pilgrimages to that place, was always received into the house of Mr. and Mrs. Sori: who had prevailed on him to accept of a little apartment. We we will therefore give their depositions word for word as they are contained in an authentic Act drawn up by a Notary to serve in the Process of his canonization. "In " the latter days of the last Lent (*say they*, " *that is, Mr. and Mrs. Sori*) we were " conversing about Benedict Joseph, ima- " gining that he would soon come to Lo- " retto. Our Son whose name is Joseph, " and is only five years and four months " old: then said, *Benedict will not come*, " *Benedict is dead.* And every time that " we mentioned our expectations of seeing " Benedict Joseph Labre, he always said " the same things; *Benedict will not come at* " *all, Benedict is dead.* One day we asked " our Son, how he came to know that Be- " nedict would not come? To which he " answered: *My heart tells me so.* And " the same question being frequently pro- " posed to him, always received the same " answer: *My heart tells me so.*" Mrs.

Mrs. Sori, in her depofition fays: " On
" Maunday Thurfday in this fame year, I
" faid thefe very words. *This is the day*
" *that Benedict is to come: I muft get his*
" *little apartment ready for him:* and my
" Son Jofeph, who heard me fay thofe
" words, immediately replied: *I have al-*
" *ready told you that Benedict will not come*
" *at all. Benedict is gone to Heaven.*"

What happened in Rome at the time of
the death of this Servant of God, is by no
means lefs furprifing. God, who is fometimes pleafed to make infants the publifhers
of his wonders and of the glory of his
name: feems to have ordained that they
fhould be his firft Heralds to announce the
glory of his Servant. Scarce had this poor
follower of Jefus Chrift breathed out his
laft; but all at once, the children of the
houfes that were near that of Mr. Zaccarelli filled the whole ftreet with their noife,
crying out with one accord, *The Saint is
dead, The Saint is dead.* And on the following morning the fame exclamations and
the fame words were repeated both in the
fame ftreet, and in the fquare or broad place
before the Church of S. Mary di Monti.

But prefently after, they were not only
young children who publifhed the fanctity
of Benedict; but the people, and all Rome
joined their voices, and repeated the fame
words; *A Saint is dead.*

Great

Great numbers of perfons, who have been eminent for their holinefs, and famous for their miracles, have ended the days of their mortal life in this great City: but the death of none of them ever excited fo rapid and lively an emotion in the minds of the people, as the death of this poor beggar: this excited a kind of univerfal commotion. For in the ftreets hardly any thing could be heard but thefe few words. *There is a Saint dead in Rome; which is the place where the Saint died. ?*

The people ran in fuch multitudes to the houfe of Mr. Zaccarelli, that he was forced to permit them to enter; but a guard of Corfican foldiers was called to keep off the crowd, and preferve good order.

The inhabitants of this quarter being defirous of fecuring to themfelves the poffeffion of his precious remains, begged that he might be buried in the Church of S. Mary di Monti: for this was the Church which during his life, Benedict had moft freqented: and it may with truth be faid, that from the time that he had fixed his refidence in Rome, he had paffed the greateft part of his life in it. But the Rector of S. Saviour's Parifh infifted on having it buried in his Church. This oppofition which they met with, made them fet their heads to work, and they foon difcovered that Benedict was an inhabitant, not of the Parifh of St. Saviour, but of S. Mari

di

di Monti. To the Rector therefore of this Parish they petitioned for this favour, which he readily granted. And the Rector of the Church of St. Mary di Monti being assured of the necessary licence: concurred with the wishes of his zealous Parishioners, and prepared for the funeral obsequies of the Servant of God, which were performed at the expence of his friend Mr. Zaccarelli.

The people now impatiently expecting the removal of his body: the crowd kept continually increasing, the guard was doubled and the soldiers who accompanied the Corpse kept the people in good order and at the same time composed a kind of funeral procession.

From the moment that the Corpse went out of the house, to the end of the burial-service, a sight was seen which is very difficult to be described. Some joined their voices with the fingers of the Church; and published the praises of the Servant of God; others in a loud voice extolled the happiness of his dying such a precious death. These shed tears of devotion in abundance; and the others, tears of compunction. The interiour grace of God at the same time mixed itself in some manner with the first impressions which this spectacle made upon their senses. Many great sinners perceived themselves agitated and troubled in mind at the consideration of

N   their

their paſt lives, and immediately formed reſolutions of amendment, to which may God give his bleſſing, and render effica-cious.

Theſe were the happy firſt-fruits of Souls converted at the Tomb, and by the interceſſion of this Servant of God, who for their converſion had offered up ſo many prayers, ſo many ſighs, ſo many tears, ſo many labours, and ſo many auſte-rities.

The ſolemnity of Maunday-Thurſday does not permit that any one ſhould be bu-ried at Rome on that day; for which rea-ſon the Corpſe of the Servant of God was depoſited in a place in the Church which joins to the Sacriſty.

There was no perſon in the neighbour-hood of Mr. Zaccarelli, who knew that I was Benedict's Confeſſor; ſo that it was not till the morning after his death that Mr. Mancini informed them of it: and this was the reaſon why I knew nothing of what had happened till Friday morning, when Mr. Mancini ſent me a note to ac-quaint me with it.

After the Funeral Service was over, the devotion and concourſe of people augmen-ted in a very extraordinary degree. The Cardinal Vicar gave leave to ſuſpend the laying his body in the ground for the ſpace of four days; and at the ſame time proper

precautions

precautions were taken to keep good order and prevent any tumult.

The concourse of people during thefe four days, inftead of diminifhing, feemed to increafe every hour. People of all ages, ftates, and conditions, ran, prefled into the crowd, and were confounded with each other. Perfons of the firft rank catched the eager defires of the people, and augmented it by their example. Some were feen ufing their utmoft endeavours to prefs through the crowd and get up to the Servant of God, and others kneeling down at his feet: fome with an extraordinary devotion touching his body with their Rofaries; others kiffing his hands and bathing them with their tears: and every one fhewing their furprize and admiration, when touching fometimes his hands, fometimes his feet, or any other parts of his flefh, they found them equally foft, flexible and in a ftate perfectly found and uncorrupted.

On Eafter Sunday in the afternoon which was the time appointed for interring the Body of Benedict, the Cardinal Vicar fent to the Church of St. Mary di Monti, Mr. Cofelli, one of the Canons and his Attorney General, as alfo an Apoftolical Notary and a Surgeon. They brought with them a great number of perfons to be witneffes of their proceedings, who by their quality, age and condition were thoroughly capable of at-

tefting

testing and giving authenticity to the acts which they should have to draw up, in consequence of the most rigorous examination. And by the particular account of their proceedings, every one may see with what wisdom and prudence they executed their commission.

It appears evident both from the informations which they took, and from their own observations, and experiments many times repeated both by them, and by the witnesses, that the body did not exhale the least disagreeable smell or shew any sign of putrefaction: but on the contrary that the flesh was perfectly flexible and elastick in the same manner as is the flesh of a living man who is in a state of good health.

We have judged it proper here to relate several other particularities relative to the flexibility and incorruption of the body of Benedict, though without pretending to have them considered as absolutely miraculous, unless they should hereafter acquire that certainty and authority, in consequence of a more thorough and perfect investigation and examination of the facts.

We have before mentioned the two tumours or swellings which covered both the knees of the Servant of God: as likewise the cause from whence those swellings arose: and the excrutiating pains which he must necessarily have suffered in consequence of these swellings.

God

God put it into their minds immediately to examine thefe fwellings, in the knees of Benedict. They found the two fwellings were like two globes of a confiderable fize: but the flefh was fo flexible and elaftick, that when any one had preffed them with his finger, he faw them immediately return to their original form of themfelves, and that by the mere action of the mufcles. This Phenomenon was in every refpect like that which is obferved in preffing the flefh of a living man. A great number of perfons were convinced of this by trying the experiment. And I myfelf have my own experience for my voucher, becaufe I many times tried the experiment; and always with equal fuccefs.

Another thing which we have to fpeak of, and which feems no lefs extraordinary, has been attefted by many perfons, and particularly by F. Francis Bagnagatti one of the members of the Congregation of pious labourers. On Thurfday at night the body of Benedict was all over in a fweat, and that in fuch abundance that his face appeared to be bathed and covered with it. Brother Bagnagatti who related to me this fact, wiped the face of Benedict with the Capuche with which his head was covered. The Capuche was thoroughly wetted with his fweat. This Capuche I carefully keep in my poffeffion, and it retains very plainly the ftains made in it by the quantity of

N 3

fweat

fweat which it had imbibed and with which it was entirely penetrated. The fame Phenomenon happened again on Saturday and has been certified by many eye-witneffes, who more fully to convince themfelves applied their hands to his face.

But now returning again to the fubject of this narration, we fhall give an account of a third extraordinary thing which is ftill more aftonifhing than the two former. And to obferve the moft exact fidelity, we will do little more than tranfcribe the verbal Procefs drawn up by the Commiffary, of the Cardinal Vicar at the very place, and at the very moment when it happened, in the prefence of a great number of perfons who were eye-witneffes of the fact.

After they had, by many obfervations and repeated experiments, examined and proved the ftate of incorruption, and flexibility of the limbs and flefh of the Servant of God: they thought of changing his cloaths, and putting on him a white habit, which is the peculiar drefs of the members of the Society of S. Mary ad Nives, to which fociety they had affociated him after his death. And the body having till this time lain ftretched out upon two benches, which being placed clofe to each other formed a kind of Table: in order to put on this habit, it was neceffary to lift him up, and place him in a fitting pofture. Francis Bagnagatti holding him in this
pofition

pofition by the fhoulders, Benedict ſtretch-
ed out his left hand, and laid hold on the
board of one of the benches, as if he wanted to fupport his body from falling after its
being in a natural and proper attitude for
this purpofe. The body was furrounded
on all fides by a great number of fpectators: I myfelf was ſtanding at his feet, and
then had my eyes turned towards a table
where a perfon was tranfcribing a Note or
Memorial in Latin which afterwards was
to be enclofed in a cafe of led, and placed
in the Coffin of Benedict.

At the noife which I heard on all fides,
and the figns of aftonifhment which I perceived in every countenance, I turned my
face towards Benedict, and was no lefs
furprifed than the other fpectators when I
obferved the attitude of his body at that
time.

Some of the witneffes being defirous of
being fully affured whether what had happened, and which appeared marvellous,
might not proceed from a natural caufe, or
be the effect of mere chance: they defired
that the body fhould be inclined a little
more to the left fide. This experiment
was tried accordingly. If the hand and
fingers had been no more than fimply
applied to the bench; if the mufcles had
not been in a ſtate of tenfion and real con-
traction; then when the body was more
inclined to the left fide, the hand would
naturally

naturally follow the motion and inclination of the body, and by its own weight loofen and fall lower than the bench: but inftead of this, which was natural and neceffary, the hand remained fixed to the board of the bench at the fame place, till fuch time as the by-ftanders loofened it.

They did not confine themfelves to this firft experiment; they repeated it over again and again, and as often as it was repeated, the fame Phenomenon appeared. For one of the affiftants having required that the hand fhould be loofened from the bench, and the body placed again in its former attitude: after that in confequence of this requifition, it was again in a fitting pofture; and the eyes of all the fpectators were fixed upon the body of Benedict in expectation of what might happen, and I myfelf was particularly attentive to that fame hand: we faw the body naturally fupporting itfelf, in the fame manner as we had feen it fupport itfelf before: and in like manner the hand holding faft by and fqueezing the bench, in fuch manner that the thumb and palm of the hand preffed upon the top of the bench; and the fingers were clenched underneath it, the body performing and reprefenting the action and attitude of a living man.

Some time after this, they loofed his hand, and were convinced of the reality of
the

the flexibility of his fingers, and of the extension and play of the mufcles.

I add that through the whole length of the hand, of the left arm, and even to the middle of the breaft on the fame fide; the fame contractions, and the fame play was obferved in all the mufcles, as might have been obferved in any living perfon, who wanting to fuftain the weight of his body in the fame attitude, fhould feize hold on any thing that was in his way to ferve him as a prop.

By a prudent precaution, the Notary at this part of his Verbal Procefs fet down the Names and Titles of the witneffes: as likewife the names, and titles, or conditions of the principal perfons who were fpectators. The Verbal Procefs, formed in the very prefence of the witneffes was immediately committed to the Prefs, and upwards of eight thoufand Copies taken off.

Some time after when they had fatisfied the pious curiofity of thofe who were prefent: they took off his cloaths with all fuitable decency, and after cloathing him in a white habit, and wrapping him up in a proper and decent fheet, he was laid in a wooden coffin. Many perfons who were then without and who had climbed up to a fufficient height to fee between the bars what was done in the Chapel, begged with great earneftnefs that they would lift up that part of the fheet which covered the

head

head of the Servant of God, and afford
them the confolation of taking a farewell
look at his face.

This requeft was granted, and at the
fame time they placed in the foot of the
Coffin near the feet, the leaden cafe which
contained the Memorandum or Eulogium
abovementioned : and to which was affixed
the Seal of the Cardinal Vicar.

The Body of Benedict was afterwards
carried into the Church, and put under
ground near the High Altar, on the Epiftle
fide. They chofe this place in the Church
by the confent and leave of the Cardinal
Vicar.

The putting the body under ground did
not in the leaft diminifh the concourfe of
people. They came with the fame eagernefs to render to him at his tomb the fame
refpect and veneration which they had rendered to his body whilft it continued to be
publickly expofed to the veneration of the
Faithful.

On Eafter-Monday an immenfe multitude of people affembled from every quarter of Rome, at the report of the extraordinary favours, which God, to honour his
Servant, had beftowed on a great number
of people who had implored his interceffion. The number of the Soldiers that
were appointed to keep good order, were
increafed, but all to no purpofe. The una-
voidable tumult, occafioned by fuch a great

concourfe

concourfe of people, obliged them to give
over celebrating the Maffes and Divine
offices. And alfo laid them under a neceffity of removing the Bleffed Sacrament,
from the High Altar to an inner Chapel.

Some days after when it was found that
the moft prudent precautions were infuf-
ficient to reftrain the multitude: an Order
came from the Superiors, to fhut up the
Church: and an exprefs prohibition a-
gainft opening it for any perfon whom-
foever. And Soldiers were placed continually on the outfide to guard the door:
this new precaution was judged neceffary
to prevent the heat of an indifcreet
zeal.

The Order of the Superiors was obeyed:
but the Church did not ceafe continually
both by day and by night to be furrounded
by a great multitude of perfons: fome of
whom prayed on their knees in the adjacent ftreets: and thofe who could approach
nearer knelt down at the foot of the walls.

The church continued fhut for two
whole days; and it was thought they might
now take off the prohibition, without danger of any inconvenience refulting there-
from. But as foon as ever the rumour was
fpread of the Church being opened again,
crowds of people began to reaffemble, fo
that it was neceffary to form an inclofure
round the Tomb, and keep off the people
by a balluftrade: round which a fufficient

number of soldiers were placed to prevent any disturbance. This guard was judged necessary, and continued by the Tomb of the Servant of God, for the space of two months.

The news of his death, and the report of the circumstances that accompanied it, and of the wonders which God had wrought at his Tomb, was spread through every Province with an incredible rapidity.

The devotion of Foreigners now began to unite with that of the inhabitants of Rome. And now a new concourse of people arrived from all parts, and some from the most distant Provinces. Some came to petition for temporal or spiritual favours through the intercession of this poor follower of Jesus Christ: others to pay their veneration at his Tomb, or to return thanks to God for miraculous cures wrought upon them, or for some interior or exterior favours which they declared they had received from God by his merits and intercession.

If we consider well the extraordinary facts which preceded and accompanied these miraculous cures, which fame has published throughout all parts, if we consider the cures in themselves, their number, their different kinds, the variety and great distance of the places where they were performed; and all the other circumstances which prove their truth and their authenticity;

thenticity: how incredulous foever a man may be, he will find it extremely difficult to refift that conviction which naturally follows from the multitude, the authority, and combination of their proofs.

It is true, that till the Church has pronounced its decifion, we ought to fufpend our judgment concering them. Prudence ought to curb the hafte of an indifcreet zeal. And the proofs not having yet been examined and approved by lawful Authority, is a fuficient reafon for us not to publifh them as inconteftible miracles. But this at leaft we may affirm, and that without any fear of being charged with precipitation and rafhnefs, that the truth of a great number of extraordinary cures is founded upon the ftrongeft prefumption imaginanable.

For of what kind of cures do we now fpeak? Of cures which are as aftonifhing by their multitude, as by their variety: of cures of diforders fpread through all the members of the human body, and all the organs of the fenfes: and in many inftances, of long infirmities, of diforders of ten, twenty, and thirty years continuance, and to which fome had been fubject even from their very birth. We here fpeak of diforders, whofe exiftence was unqueftionable, and cure inftantaneous. We have thought proper here to fhew our reader how long a lift of them might be made out, if we were to give a particular account of each of them. For we fee that cancers have been cured, fiftulas, epilepfies, gangrenes, mortifications, rickets, fchirrus, wens, impofthumes, dropfies, apoplexies, ulcers, confumptions, afthmas, fcurvies, blindnefs, deafnefs, fractures, and broken limbs.

We fpeak moreover of wonderful cures, publifhed not only at Rome, but in a multitude of places far diftant both from this Capital, and from each other; that is to fay; at Naples, Genoa, Malta, Milan, Bergame, Capua, Peruggia, Boulognia, in the County of Venaiffin, in France, and in a great number of other places which would be too tedious now to enumerate.*

We

* The different places where, fince the month of Auguft laft paft, accounts of miraculous cures have been publifhed, without mentioning Rome, are at Urbino, Perugia, Fermo, Mocerato, Recanato, Loretto, Camerino, Cefenne, Orviette, Ancona, Toligno, Velletrie Riete, Montefiafcoune, Monte-Sancto, Narni, Civita-Vecchia, Gubbio, Tolentino, Fabriano Urbanio, Montalboddo, Heltanno, Cafcia, Capoue, Caprarola, Ncozanno; in the Diocefs of Nep, Maffa-Lombarda, in the Diocefs of Imola, Stipès; in the Diocefs of Rieti, Selci, Monte-Lupore; in the Diocefs of Loretto, Monte-Rolondo, Monte-Perzio, Monte-Tanico, Vitralla; in the Diocefs of Viterbo, Anguillara; Diocefs of Sutri, Siterna, Diocefs

We fpeak thirdly with regard to many of
them, that they are cures the accounts of
which are accompanied with Certificates
of Phyficians, and other intelligent perfons, who atteft both the former naturally
incurable ftate of the patients, and the fudden tranfition from that ftate to a ftate of
health, as likewife the permanency of the
cure. And fome of which accounts are
accompanied with the teftimony of the
perfons themfelves on whom thofe miraculous cures were wrought, and who attribute
the recovery of their health to the interceffion of Benedict, whom they had invoked to intercede with God in their behalf.

In a word we here fpeak of cures that
have been performed, not fucceffively in a
long tract of time; but fuch as have been
performed in a very fhort fpace: and fo
fpeedily that it cannot by any means be
faid that the enthufiafm of one city has
been produced by the enthufiafm of the

O 2   other

Diocefs of Velletri, Capo-di-Monte; Diocefs of
Monte Siafcone. And out of the Ecclefiaftical
State, at Geneva, Malta, Milan, Bergame,
Naples; and in thefe different States, Barrs,
Capua, Aquila, Mont Royal, Amatrice, A-
vezzanno, Petreto, Sperlongay, Roccadi, Bot-
tes, la Sante Marie, Capiftrello, Arce, in France,
Bolene, in the County of Venaiffin, at many places
in Artois; at Aix in Provence, Lille, Cavaillon,
and many other places.

other places where these extraordinary facts have happened.

Accounts of cures were published at Rome in the very week in which the Servant of God departed out of this life. In all the other places, where similar cures have been performed, many of them have been performed immediately after the news arrived of what had been done at Rome.

For the first three months after the death of Benedict, scarce a week has passed, in which there has not been at Rome some verbal processes of miraculous cures : or in which some people on whom miraculous cures have been performed, have not arrived to publish at the Tomb of this poor Servant of Jesus Christ, both his Fame, and their own gratitude to God for the benefits bestowed on them by his intercession.

By a singular disposition of divine Prudence, the particulars of his life, from his infancy to his death, have been known, published, and proved in so ready a manner, and at the same time with such exactness, that this itself may justly be looked upon as a very extraordinary thing. From hence they passed on from admiration at the wonders attributed to his intercession, to admiration at his virtues : and these two causes united, confirmed, and more and more contributed to extend the reputation of his sanctity, which immediately was spread

throughout

throughout all Europe with an incredible rapidity.

As God was pleafed to make the glory of Benedict fhine every day by new favours: the Cardinal-Vicar thought it a duty incumbent on him to give his orders to commence the preliminary proceedings, which always ferve as an introduction to the Procefs of the Beatification and Canonization of Saints. And therefore he publifhed his orders to begin the folemn Formalities, prefcribed by the Popes Urban the Eighth and Innocent the Ninth.

The Archbifhop of Neocefarea was delegated in the month of May 1783, to receive the Juridical Informations relative to thofe miraculous cures: and examine the witneffes who fhould appear for this purpofe and who were to declare upon oath the truth of the facts which they afferted.

The Rev. F. Palma Rector of the Church of S. Mary di Monti where Benedict was buried was nominated to do the bufinefs of Solicitor in the caufe. The Canon Cofelli Attorney-General of the Vicariate of Rome was appointed to do the bufinefs of Proctor: and Mr. Cicconi, that of Secretary to the Commiffion.

The informations taken at Loretto by authority of the Holy See, and thofe taken in France, where the Servant of God was born, by the Bifhop of Boulogne, have been already remitted to, and received by

O 3   the

the Congregation of Rites: and the Process is now carrying on with the utmost diligence and success.

As obedient children of the Church, we ought to wait its decision with respect. Every thing concurs to afford us hopes that these words of Solomon will be fully verified in the person of this poor follower of Jesus Christ. *There is a whithered man that wanteth help, is very weak, and full of poverty, Yet the eye of God hath looked upon him for good, and hath raised him up from his low condition, and hath exalted his head: and many have wondered at him, and have glorified God.* Ecclus. xi. 12, 13.

THE VERBAL PROCESS.

Begun on Easter Sunday, five days after the death of the Servant of God, and immediately before the Burial of his body.

AT the request of Mr. Cajetan Palma, Superior of the Congregation called by the name of Pious Labourers, and Rector of the Church of S. Mary di Monti at Rome, I the under signed Notary Publick, accompanying Mr. Luke Anthony Cofelli, Canon, Attorney General, and Secretary of the Court of the Vicariate of Rome, went about four o'Clock in the afternoon to the said Church of S. Mary di Monti, where being arrived, and having with great difficulty

culty entered into it by the little fide door, on account of a great multitude of people crowding on all fides, I was conducted into a paffage adjoining to the Sacrifty, and in the middle of which I found a human corpfe laid out upon benches, and cloathed with a white Robe, conformable to the Cuftom of the members of the venerable Confraternity of S. Mary ad Nives, girded with a Cord proper to this habit, having his hands placed in the form of a Crofs upon his breaft, and not exhaling any fmell, either pleafant or difagreeable.

Then, the Canon, Mr. Cofelli, acting in virtue of the authority granted to him, by his Eminence the Cardinal Mark Anthony Colonna, Vicar of Rome, ordered, that to avoid the noife infeperable from the prefence of a multitude of people, the body fhould be conveyed into the Sacrifty, contiguous to the faid paffage, which was immediately executed by the help of the Soldiers.

The door of the Sacrifty being afterward fhut, they proceeded to identify the body, in the prefence of feveral witneffes: viz. Mr. Cajetan Palma, Mr. Biagio Picillo, the Fathers, Michael Trifcitto, Francis Bagnagatti, and Camillus Simeoni, (all of them Religious of the faid Congregation of Pious Labourers.) Mr. Jofeph Marconi, M. Hannibal Albani, the moft Illuftrious Count, Mr. James Piccini, Mr. Paul

Paul Mancini, Mr. Francis Zaccarelli, and Mr. Peter Sentoli: all of whom after having seen and attentively viewed the said Corpse, affirmed upon Oath, that they knew it to be the Corpse of the Servant of God, Benedict Joseph Labre, whom they all knew perfectly well while he was living: and whose Soul they now piously believe was received into the mansions of eternal rest, on Wednesday the sixteenth day of April of the present year, which was the day of his death, and which happened in the first hour after Sun-set, in the house of Mr. Zaccarelli, which is near to the aforesaid Church of S. Mary di Monti. All which they affirm to be true and according to their perfect knowledge: they having many times spoken to, and familiarly conversed with the said Benedict Joseph Labre during his life time. To which Mr. Marconi added, that he had heard his Sacramental Confessions for a considerable space of time. And Mr. Mancini added, that he had for a long time given him a lodging at night, in the hospitium destined for the poor.

The proving the identity of the Body being finished, and performed in such a manner as to render it impossible hereafter to call it in question: Mr. Coselli considering that the Sacristy was filled with a great multitude of people, ordered the body to be wrapt up in a sheet, and carried into a private Chapel near the said Sacristy, where

being

being brought by the help of the Soldiers who cleared the way, the body was laid down at full length upon two benches, which had been previoufly prepared for that purpofe: and which by being placed clofe to each other, formed a kind of table. The body was then meafured by a Joiner, who found it to be fix palms five inches in length. After which Mr. Jofeph Chigi, a Surgeon, officially appointed for this purpofe, after many trials and experiments made by him; found that the body was foft, flexible, and elaftick, in all its parts; and had not the leaft fign of corruption : which was alfo attefted by many other perfons who were prefent, and who convinced themfelves of the truth of this fact, by their own experiments.

After they had ftripped the corpfe of its garments with all proper decency; when they came to change his fhirt, in order to do this, it was neceffary to raife up his body: which was done by the undermentioned Michael Trifcitto, Francis Bagnagatti, and Camillus Simeoni, who placed the body of the deceafed in fuch a manner, that the lower part of his body remained extended upon the two united benches, and the upper part of his body was raifed upright: fo that he was then placed in a fitting pofture. At which time it was remarked, that while F. Bagnagatti was holding the corpfe by the fhoulders, the

the body of the deceased seemed to lay
hold on the board of the bench, and in a
kind of a natural manner to support its own
weight.

Those who were present having taken
notice of this Phenomenon, were desirous
of trying whether this might not have happened by chance. For which purpose,
they inclined the body a little more to the
left side : the hand nevertheless continued
to hold itself fast to the bench, till such
time as it was loosened from it by one of
the by-standers.

The hand being thus detached and removed, the body was in like manner inclined a little towards the right, in order
to place it again in a sitting possition, when
they saw that it a second time laid hold on
the edge of the bench, so that it seemed to
support itself in the same manner as it had
done before : that is to say, having the
fingers clenched under the bench, and the
thumb and palm of the hand resting upon
the top of the bench, and by this means,
taking in every respect, the attitude in
which a living man would place himself.

Some time after they loosened and lifted up the hand, and found that the fingers
were flexible, as has been mentioned a-
bove.

This Phenomenon was taken notice of by
every one who was present ; among whom
were Mr. Palma the Rector, the brothers
Michael

Michael Trifcitto, Francis Bagnagatti, Camillus Simeoni, as likewife Mr. Jofeph Noel Dulpino of the Order of S. Vincent of Paul, Mr. Fidelis Relagliati Counfellor at Law, Mr. Marconi, Mr. Mancini, Mr. Mark Anthony Colonna, Mr. Michael Angelus Bove, Mr. Peter Paul de Lunel de la Rovere, Mr. Matthew Angeletti, and feveral others.

They then cloathed the Corpfe with a new habit, according to the manner of the Brothers of the afore-mentioned Society of S. Mary ad Nives, and likewife girded it, according to the cuftom of the faid brotherhood, with a cord proper to this Habit. And then the body being wrapped in a fheet, was laid at length in a Coffin made of Chefnut-wood, which had been prepared for this purpofe, and which was eight palms and eleven inches in length, two palms and five inches in breadth towards the head, one palm and fix inches high towards the head; and at the feet its breadth was one palm two inches and a half; and one palm and two inches in height.

At his feet was placed a leaden cafe, tied fecurely all round with a green filk ribband, fealed with red fealing-wax, with the Seal of his Eminence the Cardinal Vicar. This box contained a memorandum in form of a Eulogium written in Latin upon Parchment, which is fubfcribed both by Mr.

Cofelli,

Cofelli, and by myfelf: and it is couched in thefe words.

"In the year of our Lord 1783, being
" in the ninth year of the Pontificate of our
" holy Father Pope Pius VI, BENEDICT
" JOSEPH, fon of John Baptift Labre,
" and of Anna Barbara Grandfire, born in
" the Parifh of S. Sulpice d' Amette, in the
" Diocefs of Boulogne in France, on the
" 26th of March, 1748, after having fpent
" his youth in the conftant obfervance of a
" very good conduct, under the inftruction
" and direction of his Uncle by the Fa-
" ther's fide, who was then Rector of the
" Parifh of Erin in the fame Diocefs; be-
" ing defirous of making a progrefs in
" the practice of Chriftian virtues, and of
" embracing an auftere and penitent kind
" of life : entered into the Abbey of Sept-
" Fonts of the ftricteft obfervance of the
" Order of the Cifterfians, and was admitted
" to the exercifes of the Noviciate on the
" 28th of October 1769. But finking un-
" der the aufterities which he practifed
" in this monaftery; a ficknefs which he
" patiently endured for the fpace of two
" months, obliged him on the 2d. of June
" to quit the Religious Habit which he had
" worn with edification for the fpace of
" eight months.

" After his departure from the Abbey, -
" he undertook divers pilgrimages. His
" devotion induced him particularly to vifit
" the

" the Church of Loretto, and the Tombs
" of the Holy Martyrs S. Peter and St Paul.
" After many journeys of Piety, he fixed
" his residence at Rome, from whence he
" did not depart, but only to make every
" year a Pilgrimage to Loretto.

" In every place he gave great examples of
" Christian Virtues, of Evangelical Poverty
" which he carried to the highest degree
" of perfection, living only on alms which
" were voluntarily offered to him, without
" asking; receiving only in small quanti-
" ties what was offered to him, and distri-
" buting to other poor people part of what
" was given to him; he was a man of
" a profound humility, entertaining a fo-
" vereign contempt, both for the world,
" and for himself; performing rigorous
" penitential austerities; and spending all
" his time from the morning till sun-set
" in the Churches of this city, where he
" lived, in the exercise of continual prayer.
" He made himself famous by the prac-
" tice of all the other virtues: was esteem-
" ed and beloved by all, although his gar-
" ments and outward appearance were neg-
" lected and forbidding. A distinguishing
" character of his virtue was, an entire dif-
" regard and forgetfulness of himself, that
" he might make the love and service of
" God his only occupation.

" On the 16th of April 1783, after hav-
" ing prayed for a very long time, accord-

P   ing

" ing to his custom, he fell down through
" weakness, at going out of the Church of
" S. Mary di Monti. In consequence of a
" friendly offer which was made to him, and
" which he accepted, he was carried to the
" house of a reputable man, who lives at
" a little distance from the said Church.

" His strength gradually decreasing, the
" Sacrament of Extreme Unction was ad-
" ministered to him, and being properly
" assisted by Priests, in the very moment
" while those who were present were praying
" for him, he calmly resigned his soul
" into the hands of his Creator, in the first
" hour after Sun-set, of the same day on
" which he fell sick.

" On the morning following, his body
" was conveyed with all suitable decency
" into the said Church: and a great con-
" course of people were present at his
" Dirge, which was performed at the ex-
" pence of certain pious persons, who took
" that charitable office upon themselves.

" Immediately afterwards a kind of almost
" universal commotion communicated itself
" throughout all Rome, at the news of his
" death, which spread itself suddenly, toge-
" ther with the fame of his great sanctity.
" Then, such a great concourse of people of
" all ranks and conditions, began to crowd
" to the Church, that the Soldiers who
" had been called to keep good order, had

" a great deal of difficulty to keep the
" multitude in subjection.

" To satisfy the piety of the Faithful
" whose number increased more and more,
" his Eminence the Cardinal Vicar gave
" leave to defer the laying the body un-
" der ground till the evening of Easter
" Sunday, which in this year 1783, falls on
" the twentieth of April. This same day,
" by order of his Eminence the body was,
" about the time of Sun-set laid under
" ground, in an honourable and particular
" place of this Church."

Signed.

LUKE ANTHONY COSELLI, *Attorney
General of the Vicariate of Rome.*
FRANCIS MARI, *Notary*, at the request
of Mr. JOSEPH CICCONI.

We think we ought here to add some few
interesting Ancedotes relative to the life of
this Servant of God, which we have received from Mr. Alegiani, and which afford
us a great idea of his patience, his humility,
and the profound recollection of his Soul
in prayer.

One day as this Servant of God passed
by the Hospital Colonna, where some boys
where playing at Quoits, one of them
struck him with a stone on the left leg near
the ancle bone; the blow was so violent as
to make a great quantity of blood spout
out: nevertheless he did not discover his
pain by any sign whatever; and what is

ftill

ſtill more extraordinary, is, that he did not turn about to ſee who had ſtruck him : but continued to walk on, with the ſame peace and tranquility as before.

Another day as he was croſſing the Coliſeum, ſeeing ſome boys playing in an indecent manner, he went up to them, and his zeal being enkindled, he gave them a reprimand mixed with a good deal of ſweetneſs : but the boys took up ſtones and began to throw them at their charitable monitor, as the reward of his zeal. A man who was a ſpectator of their behaviour, ran up to defend Benedict. But the ſervant of God ſaid to him : *Let them alone, let them do what they pleaſe : for if you knew who I am, you yourſelf would throw ſtones at me with ſtill more rage than theſe boys.*

It was with the ſame unalterable peace that he endured a cruel inſult from one of his benefactors. This man had given him a Bajaco, or Italian penny, but perceiving that Benedict gave it to another poor perſon, he looked upon this action in a bad light, imagining that Benedict diſdained to accept ſo ſmall an Alms : and therefore came up to him and ſtruck him with his cane. After the death of this poor Servant of Jeſus Chriſt, he remembered the injury he had done him : and penetrated with the moſt lively ſentiments of repentance, he ran to the Church of St. Mary di Monti, to aſk his pardon, and as a token and memorial of his ſorrow,

row, he left in that Church, the guilty inftrument with which he had ftruck him.

Mr. Zitli, whofe depofitions will be examined In the Procefs of Canonization, was one of the principal witneffes of the refpect and reverence with which the Servant of God prayed in the Churches. He was in a manner annihilated in the prefence of God : having his eyes turned fometimes towards the adorable victim of our Salvation, and fometimes towards the earth, with a devotion that aftonifhed every beholder. Mr. Zitli declares, that on one day, he obferved him for feveral hours, kneeling before the bleffed Sacrament, in the Church of the Capuchins, and faw him all the time totally deftitute of motion : and abforpt in adoration and prayer to fuch a degree, that he fufpected he was dead, and went to him to jog him, and thereby difcover whether he was dead or alive.

Mr. Zitli had been Treafurer to Kouli Chan, of Perfia. This Prince having been put to death by his Nephew, Mr Zitli fled to Aftracan; and being afterwards, by the Divine Mercy, brought into the bofom of the Catholic Church; and having by his liberal Alms, and other good works, ftripped himfelf of the immenfe riches, which he had brought with him ; he is now, at ninety three years of age, maintained out of charity in a Convent of the Capuchins at Rome.

P 3 RE-

REFLECTION.

How great is the difference between the death of a good man, who, having lived in a state of contempt and obscurity, leaves behind him a bright and unsullied reputation: and the death of the unbeliever famous for his crimes and his impious publications! The first is approved by Religion, only because he has faithfully discharged every duty of the state in which he lived in the world, and is revered or honoured by her only because he was so far from renouncing the service of God to serve the world: that whatsoever he did to serve the world was all referred to the honour and glory of God, and done solely for his sake. The other acquires nothing more than an empty name, which is speedily forgotten when its author is no more. Great in the eyes of the world, he almost disdained to number the just man among his slaves: while the just man upon the dunghill blessed his peaceable obscurity, and thought himself happy in having nothing to wish for, nothing to regret, and nothing to leave behind him on earth, because he knew virtue alone gives immortality.

The infidel was only solicitous to make himself a name, the present was his only object, he forgot that every thing perished with a man except his righteousness: his
thoughts

thoughts and affections were conſtantly be-
witched by preſent objects, he was chained to the earth as if he thought he was
never to be ſeparated from it. The juſt
man penetrated with the idea of the great-
neſs of God whom he adored; became
great himſelf by the conſtant practiſe of
truth, of charity, of modeſty and diſin-
tereſtedneſs: that is, he became great in the
eyes of Religion, being ennobled by Faith.
But alas: what is now become of Faith!
Is not all Europe overrun with books of in-
fidelity and immorality, which Hell has
ſent on purpoſe to poiſon, to corrupt, and
to deſtroy it. To fruſtrate this infernal
ſcheme we need only caſt a glance on the
character of the men who attack this Faith.
For while the Chriſtian can have no other
interior motive for believing divine Revelation, than the love and deſire of practiſing the virtues which it recommends: the
incredulous can have no other real motive
for not believing it, than the love and deſire of practiſing the vices which it condemns. But, by what fatality could it
happen, that what is the ſource of virtue
ſhould be an impoſture, and that light and
truth ſhould flow from the ſink of vice.
What can theſe Infidels who falſly aſſume
to themſelves the name of Philoſophers,
oppoſe to a Religion ſo ſublime in its doctrines and ſo perfect in its Morality, that
if it was the work and invention of man
we.

we might boldly affert that man has been able perfectly to imitate the work of God *.
What,

* This fublimity of the Gofpel and the purity and excelency of its maxims, and of the perfon of Jefus Chrift, of whofe life it is a fummary, is defcribed by one of the greateft Infidels of the prefent age, John James Rouffeau, in the following words. " I muft acknowledge that the " majefty of the fcriptures fills me with aftonifh- " ment: the fanctity of the Gofpel fpeaks to my " heart. Look at all the books of the Philofo- " phers, with all their pomps and you will find " them little and mean if compared with this. " Is it poffible that a book at once fo fublime, " and fo fimple can be the production of men? " Is it poffible that he whofe hiftory is here given " fhould be nothing more than man? Is this " the tone of an Euthufiaft or an ambitious Sec- " tary? What fweetnefs, what purity in his Mo- " rals? What unction in his Inftructions? What " dignity in his Maxims; What profound wif- " dom in his Difcourfes! What prefence of mind, " what warinefs and exactnefs in his anfwers! " And what command over his Paffions! Where " is the man, where is the Sage, who knows " how to act, to fuffer, and to die, without " either weaknefs or oftentation? When Plato " defcribes his imaginary juft man loaden with " all the ignominy of guilt, though really de- " ferving all the honour and rewards of virtue; " he draws Jefus Chrift at every ftroke. The
" refemblance

What, I fay can they oppofe to it, but fome
merely apparent contradictions contained
in

" refemblance is fo ftriking, that all the Fathers
" have taken notice of it, and it is not poffible
" for any one to be deceived by it. How great
" muft be the prejudices, how great the blind'-
" nefs, of the man who durft compare the Son
" of Sophronifca with the Son of Mary ? How
" great a differance is there between the one
" and the other ! Socrates, dying without pain,
" and without ignominy, eafily fupported his
" character to the laft: and if this eafy death
" had not crowned his life, we might doubt
" whether Socrates with all his wifdom had
" been any thing more than a mere Sophift.
" They fay, he invented the Rules called Mo-
" ral Philofophy. But others had firft reduced
" thofe rules to practice: he did nothing more
" than fay what they had done : and turn their
" examples into Leffons. Ariftides had been juft
" before Socrates had faid what Juftice was.
" Leonidas had died for his Country before So-
" crates had declared it a duty to love it. Spar-
" ta was fober before Socrates praifed fobriety;
" and before he had defined virtue, Greece
" abounded in virtuous men. But from whom
" did Jefus learn that fublime and pure Mora-
" lity, of which he alone has given both the Lef-
" fons and the Examples ?--The death of Socra-
" tes peacefully Philofophing in the midft of his
" friends, is the eafieft, one can defire : that
" of Jefus expiring in torments, infulted,
" fcoffed

In the holy Scriptures which have been a thoufand times cleared up and reconciled: and old fophiftical arguments which have been confuted many ages ago, and are deferving the contempt of men, even of the moft ordinary capacity. If then Faith fhould be banifhed from amongft us; the great crime of our age will be to have quitted Religion: and the lafting reproach with all posterity,

" fcoffed at, and blafphemed by a whole people,
" is the moft horrible, one can fear. Socrates
" taking the poifoned cup bleffes the man who
" prefents it to him with tears! Jefus in the
" midft of the agonies of a moft cruel death,
" prays for his favage executioners. Yes, if the
" life and death of Socrates, be thofe of a Sage;
" the life and death of Jefus, are thofe of a God.
" Shall we then fay that the Gofpel Hiftory is a
" fiction? No, my friends, this cannot be: for
" the facts of Socrates, of which no one doubts,
" are not half fo well attefted as thofe of Jefus
" Chrift. And at beft this would be only evad-
" ing the difficulty, not anfwering it. For it
" would be more difficult, to conceive that
" many fhould combine to write fuch a book:
" than that one fhould furnifh the matter.
" Jewifh Authors would never have been able
" to hit upon either this manner of expreffion
" or this fublime Morality: and the Gofpel has
" characters of truth, fo great, fo ftriking, fo
" perfectly inimitable; that the inventor would
" have been more aftonifhing than the Hero."
Rouffeau's Emile, Tom. 3. p. 179.

posterity, will be to have abandoned it
without any shadow of reason, or rather
without any other reason than that of the
violence of our passions. Dangerous Citi-
zens, their zeal is as pernicious to publick
probity as to Faith; and to the State, as to
Religion. Base and perfidious seducers,
they constitute themselves the Apostles of
impiety for no other purpose than to inspire
the authors of their fortune and the objects of their passions with weaknesses of
which they may afterwards take advantage.
They desire to extinguish the light of Faith,
only because they fear the revival of reason
and the return of virtue. But their wicked-
ness well understood, will never be able to
deceive any but those who are willing to be
deceived. And notwithstanding the un-
restrained licentiousness and daring impiety
with which they attack Religion, it will
always take so much deeper root in virtuous Souls: as it has never had any other
enemies than men in whom an audacious
pride occupied the place of knowledge and
study, and who were disgraced, vilified,
and dishonoured by their immoralities.

Wretched stupidity! when wilt thou a-
wake out of thy lethargy. With a heart
so tender for creatures: when wilt thou
cease to be so hard and insensible towards
thy God! We see the world every moment rushing towards its dissolution, the
earth

earth laid waſte by fatal accidents which
threaten it with ruin, and we do not think
on that moment which will cut our thread
of life aſunder.

FINIS.

APEN.

Appendix.

APPENDIX.

TO THE

LIFE of the SERVANT of GOD.

BENEDICT JOSEPH LABRE.

Giving an account of the Miracles said to have been wrought by the Almighty, at the Intercession of this his Faithful Servant.

WE read in the thirteenth Chapter of the fourth book of Kings, otherwise called the second book of Kings, that the Prophet *Eliseus died, and they buried him. And the rovers from Moab came into the land the same year. And some that were burying a man, saw the rovers, and cast the body into the Sepulchre of Eliseus. And when it had touched the bones of Eliseus, the man came to life, and stood upon his feet.* Here we see a miracle wrought by Almighty God, by the means of the Relicks of his Prophet, and that, without any one's petitioning for, or even apprehending the likelihood of any such miracle being wrought

in

in favour of the deceased. After this instance of the extraordinary goodness of Almighty God, it is no wonder that the woman mentioned in the Gospel, Matt. ix. 20. *who had been troubled with an issue of blood twelve years,* should have such Faith and confidence in the goodness of God, as to *think that if she should touch but the hem of our Saviour's garment, she should be healed.* And in effect we find, that her Faith and confidence were commended and rewarded by our Saviour, by the restoration of her health according to her wish.

We read again in the Acts of the Aposties xix. 12. that *Aprons and Handkerchiefs which had touched the body of S. Paul were carried to the sick, and the diseases departed from them, and the wicked spirits went out of them.*

These instances of favours received from Almighty God by touching the bones of the Prophet Eliseus, and the Aprons and Handkerchiefs which had touched the body of S. Paul: induced the Christians in the first Ages of Christianity, to pay a particular respect and veneration for the bodies, or Relicks of the holy Martyrs: not doubting but those glorious Champions who had conquered the devil and the world, by laying down their lives for the Faith of Christ, and were admitted into the mansions of eternal bliss; would obtain similar favours from God for them, or at least *present their*

Petitions

Petitions before the throne of God, and folicit for them his fpiritual graces and benedictions. Hence we read in the Acts of St. Ignatius Bifhop of Antioch and Martyr, that being devoured by the wild beafts, nothing was left of his body, *but only fome of the bones ; which were carried to Antioch,* and given to that Church, for the Martyr's fake, as an *ineftimable treafure.* Ruinart's Acta fincera Martyrum, Sect. 5. p. 707.

When the body of St. Polycarp was burnt, the Chriftians collected what remained of his bones, and carried them away: *which they valued more than Gold and Precious Stones.* Eufebius lib. 4. Hift. cap. 15. p. 134.

When St. Andronicus fuffered Martyrdom, the Proconful Maximus commanded his tongue and teeth to be pulled out and burnt to afhes, and the afhes thrown into the wind, *left,* faid he , *any pitiful women of the Chriftians, fhould keep them for a treafure.* Ruinart. p. 487.

St. Bafil fays, that according to the Jewifh Rites, all dead bodies are an abomination : but now, *if any one dies for the Name of Chrift, his Relicks are efteemed precious. Then, the touch of a dead body defiled a man ; now it almoft fanctifies him.* St. Bafil in *Pfalm.* 115. T. 1. p. 274.

St. Gregory Nyffen fays, that a Chriftian *thinks himfelf fanctified and bleft by touching the Tomb of a Martyr : and much*

more

more if he be allowed to take away any of the dust from the Sepulchre. Orat. de St. Theodoro Mart. Tom. 3. p. 579. 580.

St. Jerom writing against *Vigilantius,* who pretended that *Relicks were not to be honoured:* opposes against him the *Example of all the Bishops in the world.* Lib. contra Vigilantium.

Again, says he, *We honour the Relicks of the Martyrs, that we may adore him whose Martyrs they are. We honour the Servants, that the Master may be honoured, who says; he that receives you, receives me.* Ep. 53. ad Riparium. And again, *You write that Vigilantius vomits once more his poison against the Relicks of the Martyrs, calling us Dust-worshippers and Idolaters, for reverencing DEAD Mens Bones. Oh unhappy man who can never be sufficiently pitied.* Ibid.

Dr. Burnet the Protestant Bishop of Salisbury says. " *It is no wonder that great care was taken in the beginnings of Christianity, to shew all possible respect and tenderness even to the Bodies of the Martyrs. There is something of this planted so deep in Human Nature, that though the Philosophy if it cannot be so well made out, yet it seems to be somewhat more than an universal custom.——We think that all decent honours are indeed due to the bodies of the Saints, which were once the Temples of the Holy Ghost.*"——And writing concerning the Acts which give an account of the respect paid by the Primitive
Christians

Christians to the Relicks of St. Polycarp, he fays, *This is one of the moſt valuable pieces of true and genuine Antiquity : and it ſhews us very fully the ſenſe of that Age, both concerning the Relicks, and the worſhip of the Saints.* Burnets Expoſ. of the 39. Articles. *Art.* 22. p. 313. 316.

And laſtly Eunapius a pagan writer who lived in the fourth century, fays. *The Chriſtians, gathering the heads and bones of ſuch as the Magiſtrates had executed, made them their Gods, proſtrated before them, and thought themſelves purer, by being defiled at their Tombs.*

This reſpect and veneration which was ſhewn to the Relicks of the Martyrs, and which was referred to and redounded to the Glory of God, whoſe Martyrs they are : was approved of by God himſelf; both by miraculouſly revealing where the Relicks of ſome of his Martyrs were depoſited, and by the many Miracles he was pleaſed to work by their means.

Concerning the Miracles wrought by the Relicks of the Martyrs, St. Gregory Nazianzen fays. " Did you not fear the " Martyrs and Saints, John, Peter, Paul, " James, Stephen, Luke, Andrew, Thecla, " and ſo many others—to whom great ho- " nour and Feſtivals are appointed, *by whom* " *devils are caſt out, and diſeaſes cured:* " *whoſe very bodies whether touched, or ho-* " *oured, do the ſame as their holy Souls : and*

Q 3   " a drop

" *a drop of their blood, or any little remnant*
" *of their Paffion; as much as their bodies.*"
Orat. 3. quæ eft 1 cont. Julianum Tom. 1.
p. 76. Ed. Paris.

St. Ambrofe fays. *You have known, nay*
yourfelves have feen many diffpoffeffed, many
delivered from their infirmities as foon as
they touched the Veil which covered the holy
Bodies. The ancient Miracles of Chrift are
renewed. You fee many cured, by the fhadow
as it were of the Saints' Bodies. How many
Handkerchiefs are they touched with? How
many Veils, by touching the facred Relicks,
become inftruments of the greateft cures?
Every one is glad to touch the moft diftant
hem ; and if he does it, he will be healed.
St. Ambrofe Ep. 22.

S. Ifidore of Pelufium. *If this offends*
you that we honour the afhes of the Martyrs'
Bodies, becaufe they loved God and ferved
him conftantly; afk thofe who have been
healed by them, and enquire into the number
of diftempers from which they have been
freed. If you do this, you will be fo far from
laughing at what we do, that you will be
willing to join with us in fo innocent a prac-
tice. lib. 1. *Ep.* 55.

St. Auftin in his Book of the *City of God,*
relates feveral Miracles performed at the
Shrines, or by the means of the Relicks of
St. Stephen: viz. 1. A blind woman recovered her fight, by applying to her eyes
fome flowers which had touched his Relicks.——

licks.— 2. Bishop Lucillus, by carrying the Relicks of St. Stephen, was cured of a Fiſtula, with which he had long been troubled, and was never troubled with it after that day. —3. Eucherius, a Spaniſh Prieſt, who dwelt at Calame, was cured of the Stone by part of the ſame Relicks, which Biſhop Poſſidius carried thither : and being afterwards laid out for dead in conſequence of another diſorder : by the help of the ſaid Martyr, to whoſe Shrine they carried him, was reſtored to his former life and ſoundneſs.—4. A child which had been cruſhed by a cart, was carried by its mother, and laid down before the ſhrine of St. Stephen, where it recovered both life and full ſtrength in an inſtant.—5. A devout woman at Caſpaliana, being ſick and paſt recovery ſent her garment to the Shrine : but before it came back, ſhe was dead. However, her Parents covered her with it : which done, ſhe preſently revived, and was in as good health as ever.—6. The like happened to the daughter of one Baſſus, a Syrian who dwelt at Hippo : he covered his dead daughter with her garment which he had carried to the Shrine, and ſhe preſently was reſtored to life.—7. Irenæus a Collector, having one of his Sons dead ; one adviſed him to anoint him with ſome of St. Stephen's oil : he did ſo, and his ſon was reſtored to it.—After giving an account of theſe Miracles, St. Auſtin goes on

and

and says. *If I should write all the Miracles performed on mens' bodies, by the Memorials of St. Stephen, only at Calama and Hippo, it would be a work of many volumes, and not be perfect neither.*——*It is not yet two years since his Memory began,* (that is, his Relicks were deposited) *at Hippo, and although we ourselves do know many Miracles done there since, that are not recorded, yet there are relations given in of almost Seventy of those that have been done since that time to this.* St. Aug *lib. 22. de Civit. Dei. cap. 8.*

— Several other Miracles of the like nature are by St. Ambrose, St. Augustine, and St. Paulinus, related to have been performed at Milan, by means of the Relicks of SS. Gervasius and Protasius: and indeed S. Ambrose in the place above quoted says that the veils which touched those Relicks had *become instruments of the greatest cures.* And for the truth of those miracles appeals to those who had been eye-witnesses of them.

Theodoret mentions another practice of the Faithful in his days: for he says. *That those who ask with Faith, obtain their requests as appears from the Donaries witnessing their cures. For some hang up the resemblances of Eyes, some of Feet, others of Hands, made of Gold or Silver.*——*These shew the Martyr's Power, and that the God whom they worshipped, is the True God.* Serm. 8.

de

de curand Græcor Affect. Tom. 4. p. 593, 594.

Since then Almighty God has been pleased frequently to work Miracles by the means of the Relicks of the Martyrs, in Testimony of his Faith and of the Sanctity of his Servants, in like manner as he had before wrought the like miracles by the means of the Aprons and Handkerchiefs that had touched the body of S. Paul, in testimony of his Divine Commission and Authority to preach the same faith to all the world : it is no wonder that the Christians should entertain a great veneration for those sacred remains of those Servants of God, and present themselves before the Tombs of the Martyrs, to beg of them to intercede with God in their behalf, to beseech him to deliver them from their afflictions, and bestow upon them all the spiritual and temporal blessings of which they stood in need: as the Holy Fathers in their writings assure us they did. For St. Chrysostom says: *He who wears the Purple comes to these Tombs to kiss them; and casting off his Pride, standeth humbly, invoking the Saints, that they may defend him at the Tribunal of God. And that the Tent-maker, and Fisherman, though dead, may be his Patrons, is the earnest request of him that wears the Diadem.* St. Chrysost. hom. 26. in Ep. 2. ad Cor.

And

And in another place he exhorts the people to make this their constant practice. *Let us not therefore on this day only, but every day visit his Tomb, that thereby we may obtain spiritual blessings from God. For if by touching the bones of Elisha a dead body was restored to life, if a man approaches to the Tomb with Faith, he may with much more reason hope for blessings at present, since Graces flow with more abundance. God has given us the Relicks of his Saints, that he might lead us by degrees to an emulation of their zeal, and that we might have a security, and comfort against the evils which surround us.* Tom. 1. Or 42. p. 507.

And again. *Let us*, says he, *therefore, not only on this day, but every day, visit their Tombs,* (of Domnina, Berenice and Prosdoce whose Shrines were in the City of Antioch where he preached this Sermon) *that thereby we may obtain spiritual blessings from God. Let us beseech them, let us beg of them to be our Protectresses. For their power was great, not only when living, but is also, and much more when dead. For now they bear the marks of Christ. And when they shew these, they may obtain all things from the King.* St. Chrysost. Tom. 1, Or 51. Ed. Ben. p. 570.

St. Ambrose says: *The Martyrs are to be invoked, whose Patronage we have a*
claim

claim to, by *poſſeſſing their Relicks*.—*Let us not be aſhamed to make uſe of them as Interceſſors for our Infirmity; who knew the weakneſs of the Body, at the ſame time that they conquered it.* Lib de Viduis.

Mr. Thorndike a Proteſtant writer ſays. *It is confeſſed that the lights, both of the Greek and Latin Church, Baſil, Nazianzen, Nyſſen, Ambroſe, Jerom, Auguſtine, Chryſoſtom, both Cyrils, Theodoret, Fulgentius, Gregory the Great, Leo; more, or rather all after that time, have ſpoken to the Saints, and deſired their aſſiſtance.* Thorndike's Epil. part 3. p. 358.

And Biſhop Mountague in his Treatiſe of the Invocation of Saints p. 97. ſays. *I ſee no abſurdity in nature, no incongruity unto Analogy of Faith, no repugnancy at all to Sacred Scripture, much leſs Impiety, for any man to ſay, Holy Angel Guardian pray for me.*—And again in the ſame treatiſe he ſays of the Saints: *Could I come at them, or certainly inform them of my ſtate: without any queſtion or more ado, I would readily and willingly ſay, Holy Peter, Bleſſed Paul pray for me; recommend my caſe to Chriſt Jeſus our Lord. Where they with me, by me, in my hearing, I would run with open arms, and fall upon my knees, and with affection deſire them to pray for me.*

Hence then it appears, 1. That in the firſt Ages of Chriſtianity the Faithful preſerved the Relicks of the Martyrs with
great

great care and Veneration: looking upon them as more valuable than gold and Precious Stones.—2. That God wrought many Miracles in favour of thofe, who at the Tombs of the Martyrs touched their Relicks, and with a lively Faith implored their Interceffion.—3. That the Holy Fathers, the moft illuftrious Lights of God's Church, bear Teftimony to thefe Miracles being wrought.—And 4. the fame Holy Fathers exhort and encourage the Faithful to vifit the Relicks of the Martyrs, and to invoke the Martyrs whofe Relicks they vifit, that they may obtain by their Interceffion fpiritual and temporal bleffings from God.

Venerable Bede in the fourth Book of his Ecclefiaftical Hiftory cap. 31 and 32. gives an account of a man who was in like manner cured of a Palfy at the Shrine of St. Cuthbert: and of another who was cured of a fwelling in his Eye-lid, by touching it with fome of the hair of the fame Saint. The fame Author relates in the life of St Cuthbert, that another perfon was alfo cured of a Palfy by having the fhoes in which St. Cuthbert had been at firft buried upon his feet. *cap. 4;.*

St. Bernard fays that after the death of St. Malachias, "*his funeral rites were* "*performed: the facrifice and all things* "*were done with the utmoft devotion. At* "*the fame time a lad ftood at a diftance* "*whofe*

" whose withered arm hung down by his side,
" and was more troublesome than beneficial
" to him. Observing which, I made a sign
" to him to come to me, And taking hold of
" his withered arm, I applied it to the hand
" of the Bishop; and he restored it to life.
" For the gift of healing still remained in the
" dead body: and his hand was to the wi-
" thered hand, what Eliseus was to the
" dead man. That lad had come from a great
" distance: and the hand which he had
" brought hanging down useless by his side,
" he carried back into his own country
" whole and as capable of performing its
" functions as the other." St. Bernard in
Vita St. Malachiæ cap. 31.

In every age God has been pleased to
work similar Miracles by the Relicks of his
Saints, both to open the eyes of the incredulous, that if they will, they may know
which is his true Faith, and embrace it for
the Salvation of their Souls: and likewise
to bear testimony to the Sanctity of his Servants. A multitude of such Miracles, after
the most rigorous examination, have been
juridically proved to have been wrought
by the relicks of St. Dominick, St. Francis, St. Anthony of Padua, St. Edmund
Archbishop of Canterbury, St. Hugh of
Lincoln, St. Richard of Chichester, St.
Thomas of Hereford, St. Vincent Ferrerius,
St. Catharine of Sienna, St. Francis Xavier,

St. John Francis Regis, and a multitude of other Saints.

Having now given a sufficient account from the testimony of the most Illustrious writers of the Church of God, of the Miracles which the Almighty has been pleased to work by the Relicks of his Saints, for the Confirmation of his Faith, the manifestation of their Sanctity, and the relief of those who with a lively Faith solicited them to become their Patrons and Intercessors before the throne of God; I come now to give an account of some of the numerous Miracles, said to have been performed at the Tomb of the Venerable Benedict Joseph Labre, in favour of several of those, who with the like lively Faith implored his intercession. The earliest account of which I find expressed in a Letter dated the 23d, of April 1783, that is, only seven days after the decease of this Servant of God, and which was written by the Vicar General of that Branch of the Order of Franciscans called the Recollects, to the Superior of the Convent of the same Order at St. Omer's of which the following is an Extract.

"Reverend Father.—I think it a duty "incumbent on me to acquaint you that a "young man, named Benedict Joseph "Labre died at Rome on Wednesday in "Holy Week, in the Odour of Sanctity. "The Miracles which he still continues to
work,

" work, draw to his Tomb an infinite num-
" ber of people who publish these wonders.
" The Blind see, the Deaf hear, the Dumb
" speak, the Lame walk, and the Para-
" liticks are healed: such are the prodigies
" which our good God works every day by
" the Intercession of this holy man. I
" should be very glad to know whether the
" Father and Mother of this good man are
" still living."

Another letter from the same person
dated the 30th of April 1783, adds.—
" There has been so great a tumult in the
" Church of S. Mary di Monti, that they
" have been obliged to shut it up."

Copy of a Letter from the Abbe de
Lunel directed to Mr. Labre, Rector of
Erin, whom the writer thought to be still
living, dated at Rome April 27th, 1783.

" Sir I think it my duty to communi-
" cate to you the following particulars
" which relate to your Nephew, who died
" like a true Saint: as he always lived
" conformable to the instructions and
" education which he received from you.
" I assure you on the word of a Priest, that
" on Easter Sunday, while they were put-
" ting on him a kind of white Rochet
" adorned with red ribbands, I was surpri-
" zed with a something, which I know not
" how to express; he with his left hand
" supported himself in a sitting posture, and
" seemed to me to be just ready to speak.

R 2   " I then

" I then began to think that he had only
" been in a trance. Every one cried out :
" A Miracle! Many of the moſt reſpectable
" perſons have aſſured me, that on Thurſ-
" day morning, the day after, his death,
" they ſaw him ſweat. His Confeſſor has
" told me, and he ſays the ſame to every
" body, that one day obſerving his
" Prayer-Book was in a very bad condi-
" tion, he thought of giving him another,
" but afterwards altered his mind, for rea-
" ſons known to himſelf. The good Peni-
" tent the next time he went to confeſſion,
" ſaid to him : *You had a mind to give me*
" *a book, and afterwards you changed your*
" *mind ; you do well : and I ſubmit.* The
" Confeſſor who had never mentioned
" it to any body, was aſtoniſhed at his
" words. The ſame thing happened to him
" concerning an Alms which he had a mind
" to beſtow upon him. But afterwards
" reflecting that this might inſpire him with
" motives of gain he changed his mind.
" At the next Confeſſion the Penitent ſaid
" to him in an innocent tone ; *You had a*
" *mind to give me an Alms : and afterwards*
" *you would not.* The Confeſſor quite
" confuſed ſaid : *Spiritual Alms is far bet-*
" *ter. That is true,* ſaid the Penitent.
" And as the Confeſſor ſaid it quite con-
" fuſed, with his hand in his pocket : *If*
" *you have a mind.—No,* ſaid the Penitent,
" *never give me any thing.* Towards the
" end

" end of April laſt year, he came all in a
" tremble to look for his Confeſſor, and
" ſaid to him. *Oh, Father, I thought that*
" *I was dead; that they had buried me at*
" *St. Mary di Monti on the Epiſtle ſide of*
" *the Altar; that there was a great multi-*
" *tude of people round my wretched body,*
" *who made a great noiſe: and that Jeſus*
" *Chriſt ſaid to me:* I GIVE YOU MY
" PLACE, AND I GO AWAY. In re-
" peating theſe words, *I go away*, he burſt
" into tears. The Confeſſor comforted
" him, and told him that was impoſſible,
" but that he had not ſinned by thinking
" ſo. But as the Confeſſor was ſtruck
" with this revelation, and he, in conſe-
" ſequence of what he heard from Benedict,
" at that very moment formed in his own
" mind an imagination of what he now
" ſees: and as, after what had paſſed be-
" tween him and his penitent concerning
" the book, and the alms, which I have
" before mentioned, he looked upon this
" man as a Saint: he went to three of the
" moſt reſpectable perſons in Rome, and
" begged they would write down this
" revelation made to one of his penitents,
" and that they would alſo atteſt it after-
" wards, if occaſion ſhould ſo require: at
" the ſame time declaring that he himſelf
" did not know what it might mean. On
" holy Saturday, when he deſired me to
" read ſome papers belonging to Benedict,

R 3   " the

" the contents of which he did not un-
" derstand, he said to me: *This is a holy*
" *Soul; he has told me most astonishing*
" *things; but yet there is something more than*
" *this which I cannot make out.* This he
" told me in the presence of the Superior
" of the Monastery where he was, and of
" another Religious man who assisted Be-
" nedict at his death.

" On last Easter Sunday, the Superior
" said to us: *I have a mind to present a pe-*
" *tition to the Cardinal-Vicar, and beg of*
" *him to transfer the Laus Perenne, or*
" *Forty Hours Prayer to some other Church,*
" *because the people come in crowds all the*
" *day long. The Princes, Prelates, and*
" *Cardinals, are so hindered by the crowds*
" *from coming during the day, that they can*
" *only come at two or three o'clock in the*
" *morning. (This continued to be the case*
" *till the 27th of April 1783.) All the*
" *people come in such manner to pray to God*
" *at his Tomb, that it seems as if they dis-*
" *regarded Jesus Christ: I therefore desire*
" *henceforward to free my conscience in this*
" *matter.*" The Confessor, the Father who
" assisted at his death, and I, did all that
" was in our power to hinder him from
" presenting this petition: alledging that
" this voluntarily poor man always went
" to the Churches where the *Laus perenne,*
" or Forty Hours prayer was held: and
" that this practice had contributed to the
                                    " sanctifi-

" fanctification of his foul. Notwith-
" ftanding which, the Superior procured
" an Order from the Cardinal-Vicar to
" transfer the *Laus perenne* to a Church
" juft by. We were very much furprifed
" on the Friday following, to find that the
" *Laus perenne* was not held at the Church
" of S. Mary di Monti, as it had been in
" former years. The Confeffor fubmit-
" ting to the Orders of his Superiors,
" when the was faying that part of the
" Office called *None*, and had come to
" thofe words of the Pfalm : *Give me un-*
" *derftanding according to thy word :* he
" publickly declares, that all at once this
" thought ftruck into his mind : " Here
" is the explication of Benedict's predic-
" tion. They have four days ago removed
" the Bleffed Sacrament out of the Church;
" and they have transferred the *Laus pe-*
" *renne* to another Church, to give free
" fcope to the devotion of the people, and
" prevent any irreverences which other-
" wife might poffibly happen : this is what
" was meant by thofe words of Jefus
" Chrift, *I give you my place.* That this is
" the meaning of thefe words, appears
" very evident to me : and indeed the
" whole city is of the fame opinion. This
" I was informed of by the Confeffor him-
" felf, who can have no intereft in deceiv-
" ing us; and moreover by the precaution
" which he took, he has proper witneffes
" of

" of the prediction. I beg you will get an
" exact account of the first part of this
" hidden life made out. Tomorrow I
" shall translate all his papers. I am, &c.

" Abbé de LUNEL.

" P. S. The devotion of the Faithful
" appears to be greater than that which the
" people shewed at the death of S. Philip
" Nerius. I am informed that the supe-
" riors intend to try this devotion for some
" days, by ordering the Church doors to
" be shut up for eight days: that they may
" see whether the people will at the expi-
" ration of that time return with the same
" fervour. None are admitted at present
" but the sick. The Sacristy is full of
" crutches and bandages."

*Extract of a Letter written by a Physician
at Rome, to his Sister, a Carmelite Nun at
Cavaillon, dated May 1, 1783.*

" A poor Frenchman, named Benedict
" Joseph Labre, died on the 16th of last
" month in the house of a charitable per-
" son who had taken him in. On the fol-
" lowing morning they were very much
" surprised to find that his limbs were
" supple and flexible, as if he had been
" only asleep.——The miraculous effects of
" his intercession, have been so rapid and
" so numerous, that to satisfy the zeal of
" the

" the people whom a strong guard of fol-
" diers is scarce able to keep in good order,
" they left the body expofed to public
" view for the fpace of four days. All
" which time the body preferved the
" flexibility, and frefhnefs of a living man.
" —After his burial an extraordinary
" concourfe of people affembled from all
" parts of Rome and the adjacent places,
" which ftill continues, and even till this
" moment they vifit the tomb of this bleffed
" man, who inceffantly works miracles in
" favour of thofe who with faith invoke
" his interceffion. The dumb fpeak, the
" blind fee, and thofe who had loft the
" ufe of their limbs, walk freely, and re-
" turn to their own houfes without any
" affiftance, and dropfical people are cured
" in an inftant. Laft Sunday a poor wo-
" man who had the dropfy, was carried
" in the fight of all the people, and laid
" upon the ftone which covers his tomb,
" when they immediately faw a great
" quantity of very fetid water come out of
" her feet, and in a moment after, fhe
" found herfelf perfectly cured. Broken
" limbs are reftored, and inveterate ulcers
" healed in an inftant. In a word, cripples
" procure themfelves to be carried and
" laid on his tomb, and they return full of
" ftrength, and as active as if they had ne-
" ver been out of order. This is a fight
" which is repeated every day, and of
                                    " which

" which the whole city of Rome are eye-
" witnesses. I cannot describe to you how
" much this excites their surprize and ad-
" miration. The incredulous, as well as
" others, melt into tears on these occasions.
" I myself have heard several make this
" acknowledgement. *I could not believe*
" *what was said concerning miracles; I have*
" *been curious, I have been to see them with*
" *my own eyes, and now I am convinced.*
" What a triumph is this for Religion!

" No one has ever seen such things as
" these. There are people who, without
" thinking of eating, from the morning
" even till night, never quit the place they
" get possession of as soon as the Church
" doors are opened; in order that they
" may be eye-witnesses of the miracles
" which are performed every instant."

" From the time of his death to this
" day, they reckon up sixty three miracles
" of the first magnitude. Among the rest,
" there is one of a young woman of twenty
" two years of age, who was born dumb,
" and who all at once obtained the use of
" her tongue; they are now teaching her
" the language, and she pronounces dis-
" tinctly every thing that they want her to
" say."

Extract

Extract of a Letter from the Abbe de Villiers, Gentleman to his Eminence Cardinal André Corsini, to his Friend, dated May 3, 1783.

" I do not know whether the public
" papers at Paris have announced the
" death of a Pilgrim born in Picardy, who
" lately died in the Odour of Sanctity:
" His name is Benedict Joseph Labre:—
" He lived a very mortified and penitent
" life; he eat no more than five or six
" ounces of bread per day, to which he
" added some peelings of lemons and
" oranges which he picked up on the
" dunghills; he drank nothing but water
" mixed with a little vinegar: his cloath-
" ing consisted of an old great coat, which
" was the same that he wore when he left
" the Abbey of Sept-Fonts in the year
" 1770, and a cord, which served him for
" a girdle; he never would accept, either
" new shoes, or new stockings: he never
" asked alms, but he received what was
" freely offered to him, provided it did
" not exceed a half sol, or half-penny:
" the *Miserere* Psalm was his favourite
" prayer: he had no fixed habitation, but
" he slept in an Hospitium of Pilgrims to
" whom he distributed the few alms he
" received: he spent the greatest part of
" the day in the Church in prayer, and in
" a kind

" a kind of extacy: he difcovered people's
" fecret thoughts, of which his Confeffor
" is an inconteftible witnefs: he foretold
" the day and hour of his death, as like-
" wife the place where he fhould be bu-
" ried, and feveral remarkable circum-
" ftances which are now verified; and
" which he declared to his Confeffor un-
" der the greateft fecret; his Confeffor's
" name is *Marconi*."——Then giving an
account of the manner of his death as is
before mentioned he goes on.—"The Re-
" ligious of the houfe where he firft fell
" down in a fit, and who are a kind of
" Miffionaries, carried his body to their
" Houfe, took poffeffion of his papers,
" and having learnt the motive of his re-
" fiding at Rome, and receiving other in-
" informations concerning the regularity
" and holinefs of his life, petitioned to
" have his body in their Church, as being
" the place where he commonly prayed,
" which was granted to them. He was
" placed in a paffage leading to the
" Church where he remained expofed till
" Eafter-Sunday in the afternoon, when he
" was buried in a feparate place by order
" of the Cardinal-Vicar: who took the
" precaution to order that the coffin in
" which his body, which was then flexible,
" was enclofed, fhould be fealed, they
" were obliged to fend a guard of foldiers
        guard the Church, and the body of
                                    " the

" the deceafed, and to keep good order.
" They formed a Juridical Verbal Procefs
" of all that had happened, and they put
" an authentick copy of it into the coffin
" with the body. The concourfe of peo-
" ple continues even to this very moment.
" The doors of the Church, and the place
" where he is buried, is ftill guarded by
" foldiers. It is imagined they will begin
" the ordinary procefs concerning the vir-
" tues of the deceafed, as foon as poffible :
" that they may afterwards proceed to ex-
" amine the miraculous cures which are
" attributed to his interceffion ; and of
" which they are now preparing the me-
" morials."

*Extract of a Letter from an Englifh Gentle-
man at Rome, to his Correfpondent in
England; dated May 10, 1783.*

" We have lately loft here an extraor-
" dinary poor man : his name was Bene-
" dict Jofeph Labre.—His fole patrimony
" was the free unfolicited charity of the
" well difpofed. He never afked alms,
" and never would take any thing above a
" bajacco, which is little more than our
" half-penny. If more was offered, he in-
" variably refufed it. This was fometimes
" rafhly imputed to greedinefs of expec-
" tation, and impatience of difappoint-
" ment : and as rafhly a Surgeon once

" ftruck

" for the future, upon the teftimony of
" man, or any number or credibility of
" men."

" Neither did this conflux of people con-
" fift entirely of the lower claffes: fome
" of the firft quality mingled with the
" crowd to vifit the fepulchre of the once
" defpifed Benedict. To fay nothing of
" fo many other great names, Cardinal de
" Bernis went to S. Mary di Monti to in-
" form himfelf on the fpot of the merit of
" his departed countryman, and pay his
" refpects to his memory; and before he
" left the Church, gave orders for the body
" to be inclofed in a lead coffin. Thus
" has God himfelf exalted the humble
" Benedict, and at the fame time his
" Church, in one, feemingly the moft con-
" temptible of her children."

*Extract of another Letter from the fame
English Gentleman, to the fame Correfpondent, dated May 21, 1783.*

" The Tomb of the Venerable Bene-
" dict, which is yet unclofed, and covered
" only with loofe boards, guarded by two
" Soldiers, is ftill reforted to by an unex-
" ampled concourfe of people. There is
" an increafing confluence of all ranks,
" and more Coaches than ever. Great
" numbers of cures are currently, and cre-
" dibly reported to be obtained, not only at
" the

" the vault where his remains are depo-
" fited, but also in other cities of Italy, by
" fuch as have recommended themfelves to
" his interceffion.—I have no room to give
" the particulars of thefe cures, which are
" generally deemed miraculous; though
" not yet declared fuch by authority.
" And indeed I have no inclination to do
" it without that fanction."

Extract of the fecond Letter which Mr. Fontaine *of the Congregation of* S. Vincent *of*
Paul *wrote to the Bifhop of Boulogne,*
dated June 4, 1783.

My Lord,
" Benedict continues to make a great
" deal of noife every day ;—it is faid that
" an innumerable multitude of miracles are
" wrought at his Tomb. It will take a
" great deal of time to examine them all ;
" but I have read feveral moft aftonifhing
" accounts of fome, which I would do
" myfelf the honour of fending to you if
" they did not make too great a bulk. The
" Tomb is every day vifited as it was on
" the firft day, and with the fame fuccefs.
" One thing which has happened, and
" which may be looked upon as the greateft
" and moft eftimable of all thefe miracles,
" is the converfion of an Englifh Preacher
" from Bofton, whofe curiofity having ex-
" cited him narrowly to examine the proofs

S 3   " of

" of many of the cures performed by the
" intercession of the Servant of God, is
" fully convinced of the reality of many of
" them: and in consequence of this con-
" viction, desired to be instructed in the
" Catholic Faith, and last Sunday made
" his abjuration of the errors in which he
" had been educated. It is worthy of notice,
" that this Englishman is a man of as
" great learning and penetration, as can
" be expected to be found in a man edu-
" cated in error."

Copy of a Letter from the Abbé de Lunel, *to the Bishop of Boulogne.*

My Lord,

" I was as incredulous with regard to
" what was reported concerning Benedict
" Joseph Labre, as St. Thomas was con-
" cerning the Resurrection of Jesus Christ.
" Nevertheless, three days after his death,
" I went out of curiosity to see him. I
" found him fresh, flexible, and without
" any sign of corruption. Providence
" ordained that at the sight of my band,
" (which in this country is peculiar to
" French Abbés) his Confessor, the Priest
" who assisted him at his death, and the
" Superior of the Monastery where he is,
" should desire me to read his papers
" (which they did not understand) and ex-
" plain them to them in Italian, which I
" readily

" readily undertook to do : and which has
" furnished me with an opportunity of be-
" ing many times witness to many won-
" derful things, and such as are thoroughly
" capable of curing my incredulity. This
" is one of your Flock, the holiness of
" whose life publishes the praises of his
" Pastor.—If no other person undertakes
" the work, I myself will give the Publick
" an exact abridgment of his life.—I have
" the honour to be, &c."

The Bishop of Boulogne, who is a Pre-
late highly distinguished both for his great
learning, and eminent virtues, in consequence of such authentick proofs of the
virtues and miracles of Benedict, who was
born in his Diocese, thought it his duty to
make his people sharers in his joy; and
therefore in a Pastoral Letter which he
published, speaks of the Servant of God
in these words.

" For the edification of the Publick
" we now take occasion to publish the ex-
" traordinary joy which is afforded to us,
" by the just motives we have to believe,
" or at least highly to presume that the
" number of the blessed inhabitants of
" Heaven have been lately increased by
" one of our subjects, who in April last,
" died at Rome in the Odour of Sanctity,
" where by living a life very austere and
" hidden with Jesus Christ in God, he was

" able

" able to say with St. Paul, whose glorious
" Tomb he frequently went to revere, *the*
" *world is crucified to me, and I to the world.*
" Although his outward appearance was
" very abject, ghastly, and forbidding to
" the eyes of men; yet his signal piety,
" his profound humility, his great love of
" poverty, joined to his generosity to the
" poor to whom he distributed the un-
" asked alms he received, had attracted the
" esteem, the good will, and the venera-
" tion of all those who know the true va-
" lue of those excellent virtues; but above
" all his assiduous and continual prayer;
" which you, O you false Sages of this
" age; endeavour so much to decry, to
" undervalue, and to destroy, as if it was
" only the contemptible practice of per-
" sons useless to Society: but cannot be
" too much defended, too much praised, or
" too much extolled. For according to a
" Divine Oracle, against which the crafty
" reasonings of human wisdom can oppose
" nothing but vain and sophistical argu-
" ments, it is very prevalent in the sight of
" him who is the sovereign Lord of times,
" of hearts, and the disposer of events."
    " Such is in substance the account which
" the Latin Eulogium gives of this vene-
" rable man: which, with the approba-
" tion of the Holy See, was put into his
" coffin: which Eulogium has been con-
" firmed by a number of letters sent from
                                " the

" the fame City: two of which were di-
" rected to us by Mr Fontaine, who hav-
" ing been for many years Publick Profef-
" for of Divinity in our Seminary, is at
" prefent at Rome tranfacting the bufinefs
" of the Congregation of S. Vincent of
" Paul. "

" Praife and glory be for ever rendered
" to the goodnefs of God, who to ftem *the*
" *torrent of iniquity*, with which the world
" is at prefent overflowed, and to provide
" antidotes to the venom of incredulity
" with which it is infected, has ordered
" that his fupernatural figns and wonders
" fhould manifeftly appear in the Capital
" of the Chriftian world: to the end that
" the general and lively fenfation which
" they have produced, fhould be more
" eafily fpread into all parts, even to the
" moft diftant regions of the world: and
" fhould moreover ferve for the triumph
" of Religion, the confufion of impiety;
" the confirmation of their Faith, and the
" encouragement of Fervour. But let
" praife and glory be rendered to him,
" particularly in this Diocefs, which is hap-
" py in having given birth to this illuftrious
" Penitent, more happy in having him for
" its fpecial Patron in Heaven: but ftill
" more happy if the relation or remem-
" brance of his heroick virtues fhall con-
" tribute to make a great number of per-
" fons imitators of his affiduous prayer;
" and

"and of his conftant endeavours to hum-
"ble himfelf, and fhall excite them to fub-
"due their paffions, *to crucify their flefh*, to
"ufe refolute efforts to bring it into fub-
"jection, and to *bear away by violence the*
"*Kingdom of Heaven*, where he now oc-
"cupies a Throne fo much the more ex-
"alted, and enjoys a degree of happinefs
"fo much the more exquifite; by how
"much more he humbled himfelf when
"on earth, and by how much more cou-
"rageoufly he *bore about the fufferings*
"*of Jefus Chrift* in his body extenuated
"with fafts and aufterities. He may now,
"like S. Peter of Alcantara, fay: *O happy*
"*penitential aufterities which have conduct-*
"*ed me to fuch, and fo great glory.* May
"we not alfo appropriate to him thofe
"beautiful texts of the Holy Scripture, as
"being verified in his perfon. *The blef-*
"*fing of God maketh hafte to reward the*
"*Juft, and in a fwift hour his bleffing*
"*beareth fruit.—There is an indigne man*
"*that wanteth help, who is very weak, and*
"*full of poverty. Yet the eye of God hath*
"*looked upon him for good, and hath lifted*
"*him up from his low condition, and hath*
"*exalted his head; and many have wondered*
"*at him, and have glorified God.—The*
"*Lord hath raifed the needy from the earth;*
"*and lifted the poor from the dunghill;*
"*that*

" that he may place him with the Princes of
" his Heavenly Court,
    " Given at Boulogne, July 3, 1783,
        " Signed,
" FRANCIS JOSEPH, *Bishop of Boulogne*,
  " By Order of his Lordship,
      " CLEMENT, Secretary."

*Letter of his Eminence Cardinal de Bernis
to Mr. Vincent Labre, Rector of La Peſſe,
Uncle of Benedict Joseph Labre.*
        " *Rome, June 9, 1783.*
   " Sir,
" I have received the letter you was
" pleaſed to write to me of the 26th of
" May, deſiring me to give you an account
" of the young Frenchman, known by the
" name of *Benedict Joseph Labre*, who
" died at Rome the 16th of April, and
" whom you ſay is your nephew. I wiſh
" it was in my power to give you a de-
" ſcription of what happened here at his
" death; but the wonders which are ſaid
" to be every day performed by his inter-
" ceſſion, and which continue till this ve-
" ry time, have attracted the attention of
" his eminence the Cardinal Vicar, who
" has ordered an account of them to be
" carefully collected, in order to examine
" into their authenticity, and the degrees
" of credit which they may deſerve. As
" your affinity with *Benedict Joseph Labre*
" has put you in a condition of being per-
                " ſonally

" fonally acquainted with him ; or at leaft
" of having a fufficient and continual
" knowledge of every thing which has
" been particularly remarkable in him dur-
" ing his life. I fhall be greatly obliged
" to you, if you will give me a particular
" account of what you have been able to
" collect concerning him, while he re-
" mained in France; as likewife all that
" you know of his travels, of his defires of
" entering into a Religious ftate; and of
" every thing elfe relating to him, from his
" birth till his arrival in Italy, and even till
" his death. I fhould be ftill more ob-
" liged to you, if you could fend me fome
" of his letters. I beg you will not leave
" any means untried of procuring fome
" of them. One at leaft is neceffary to
" prove the papers that were found about
" him after his death to be his hand-
" writing; that thereby we may know
" what he himfelf has written. I beg you
" will alfo give me an account of his fa-
" mily, their occupations, their reputation,
" and the rank they hold in Boulogne,
" where it is faid they are eftablifhed. I
" am very happy in having this opportu-
" nity of affuring you, that I am, with the
" moft perfect efteem, yours,

                    " Cardinal de BERNIS."

Extract

Extract of another Letter from the before-mentioned English Gentleman at Rome, dated June 11, 1783.

"Benedict's Miracles are now going
"through the fiery trial of Canonical Exa-
"mination : there are no lefs than eighty-
"two upon the lift : many more might be
"added : but none but the indubitable will
"ever be admitted, or approved by the
"Inqueft : and on the other hand a falfe
"modefty hinders many from fpeaking
"and giving glory to God as they ought :
"*I myfelf know a perfon cured of a diforder,*
"*which a Surgeon of the firft character po-*
"*fitively affirmed to be incurable, though not*
"*mortal, by only once vifiting the Church*
"*where his remains lay, and begging his*
"*prayers.* And yet this cure, and many
"more, if not more extraordinary, will
"never be fubjected to difcuffion. On
"Saturday I read the declaration of a
"Phyfician of Perugia, attefting the pre-
"ternatural cure of a Nun in the Bene-
"dictine Monaftery of that city, and de-
"fcribing many circumftances attending
"it, both before, and after it was obtained.
"It was in fhort thus.
    "The Gentlewoman had been crooked
"and infirm from a child, but for the two
"laft years crippled and bed-ridden to fuch
"a degree,-that fhe could not fo much as

T   "turn

" turn herſelf in her bed, nor move any
" part without diſlocating ſome joint or
" other. Nothing but diſſolution was now
" expected, and ſhe had prepared for it,
" nay wiſhed for it. At this juncture the
" report of Benedict's death, holineſs, and
" miracles, reached Perugia: and ſoon af-
" ter ſome of the many prints of him
" which are daily publiſhed in this City.
" The Abbeſs of the Monaſtery procured
" one of them, and going in ſome form
" with her Nuns to viſit the Siſter, told
" her ſhe had brought her the beggar of
" Rome to cure her; as none of her Doc-
" tors could. The poor Nun laughed at
" firſt, and then anſwered, that ſhe had ſo
" long and ſo often recommended her caſe
" to the Bleſſed Mother of God without
" any benefit to the body, that ſhe looked
" upon it to be God's will ſhe ſhould be as
" ſhe was, and that ſhe neither expected,
" nor deſired a miracle. The Abbeſs
" however held the print to her to kiſs:
" then applied it to her head, next to her
" ſhoulder, and was going on, when the
" patient ſuddenly called out, *I am well*,
" *I am perfectly well: reach my habit*.
" Being habited, ſhe went before them
" without help or ſupport to the Choir:
" continued ſome time in prayer and
" thankſgiving upon her knees, then heard
" Maſs, and at laſt joined in ſinging the
" *Te Deum* with the Community; every
" one

" one shedding abundance of tears of joy
" and exultation.—This is the substance of
" the Doctor's narrative, but divested of
" many remarkable circumstances and par-
" ticulars by him specified, as well as
" technical terms by him used: he declares
" the cure to be in every respect a perfect
" one, except it be of the Gibbosity and
" crookedness which grew with her from her
" childhood, and still remains: and he
" concludes by assuring us of his readiness
" and desire to attest the truth of every
" thing here said upon oath, unless it be
" the mode of cure, which not being an
" eye-witness to, he can only know from
" testimony. In effect, the Bishop of
" Perugia is now instituting an enquiry
" into these matters, and we shall soon see
" the Doctor's Deposition in Form.—If
" his present declaration needed any fur-
" ther confirmation, I might add, that Mr.
" Fermor of this place has a sister in the
" same Nunnery, from whom we had al-
" ready learnt the same, and some more
" singularities accompanying this stupen-
" dous transaction.

    " I must give you one little history more
" and I have done. A child of near four
" years old, three weeks ago, by an un-
" lucky fall, cut its tongue with its teeth,
" in such manner, that a large end of it,
" and part of one side hung out of its
" mouth, and seemed to hang only by a

" thread,

" thread. The poor mother almoſt dif-
" tracted, ran with it in her arms to the
" Hoſpital of our *Lady of Conſolation*,
" imagining the Surgeons might be able to
" few it up: but they ſtrongly aſſerted it
" to be impoſſible: and ſaid, they could
" only cut away the looſe part, leaving the
" other to heal of itſelf, and that the child
" muſt remain dumb. From thence ſhe
" ran to the Hoſpital of *St. Galla*, and re-
" ceived the ſame anſwer. Then return-
" ing home, and paſſing by the Church of
" S. Mary di Monti, near which ſhe lived;
" ſhe, for the firſt time, bethought herſelf
" of Benedict; and ruſhing through the
" guards, called upon him aloud to aſſiſt
" her and her child. She left the Church
" as precipitately as ſhe entered it, and
" was no ſooner within her own doors,
" than ſhe took up a print repreſenting
" Benedict at his prayers, with it touched
" the extremity of the Child's tongue, and
" replaced it in the mouth: then lulling it
" to ſleep which after ſome time ſhe ef-
" fected, and ſlipping the print under its
" cheek, ſhe retired to grieve and to pray.
" After about two hours, as near as ſhe can
" gueſs, the child awoke and called for
" Mama, and for ſomething to eat. The
" mouth being inſpected the tongue was
" found perfectly cicatrized: exhibiting
" no mark of any injury it had received,
" excepting a ſeam of a livid purpliſh caſt,
" running

" running partly acrofs it, and partly a-
" long, in the fame direction with the
" wound before. They are near neigh-
" bours of Mr. *****; and not only
" that neighbourhood, but a great part of
" Rome, is daily feeing with its own eyes,
" a living proof of Benedict's acceptable-
" nefs to Heaven —I think Thomas and
" myfelf happy in being in Rome; but
" more happy ftill in being here at fo dif-
" tinguifhed a period.

" We have juft now before us a con-
" verfion which has made a great noife
" amongft our contrymen in this city.
" The Convert was a Prefbyterian Teacher
" at Bofton in New-England, was fent
" over upon fome errand to Doctor Frank-
" lin, and though young, has travelled
" over a confiderable part of Europe,
" ftudying the modern languages with a
" view to qualify himfelf as a Profeffor of
" the fame in one of our Univerfities. At
" Rome (where he has not been long)
" without neglecting the language of the
" country, he turned his thoughts to Reli-
" gion, ftudied it in Books, canvaffed it in
" converfation with the Italians, and
" oftener with our Englifh and Scotch
" Priefts, and viewed it in all its practices
" (of which this City exhibits all its va-
" rieties) from the Pope's Chapel down to
" the Vault of Benedict. The confequence
" is that his former views are now fruf-

T 3   " trated,

" trated, and he thinks no more of fettling
" at Cambridge.—On Sunday the twenty-
" fifth of May, he made his profeffion of
" the Catholick Faith in form.—Since
" that he has made a Spiritual Retreat of
" fome days, and on Sunday the firft in-
" ftant, he made his Firft Communion.
" It is remakable that what firft (under
" God) made him begin to judge better of
" Catholicks, than he had been taught or
" taught others to do, was the behaviour
" of the French Sailors and Soldiers (not
" always the moft exemplary) at Bofton;
" having never before feen a Catholick to
" his knowledge.—He feems to be under
" very particular obligations to the French;
" for what was begun by their Military,
" one of their Mendicants has compleated
" by the Odour of his Sanctity, by the
" Iuftre of his Miracles (which were exa-
" mined by our enquirer on the fpot;) and
" by the influence of his prayers."

Extract of a Letter from the Abbé de Lunel,
dated Rome, July 16, 1783.

" ——Such things as thefe; have never
" been feen at Rome even in the moft ho-
" ly times. The Englifh and others cry
" out loudly, *It muft be acknowledged he*
" *was a good man.* With regard to his
" Miracles, the Solicitor for the Procefs of
" his Beatification, has fhewed me a lift of
" near

" near two hundred cures of all kinds of
" the moſt inveterate and incurable diſ-
" orders, that have been ſucceſſively per-
" formed; and which have been well
" proved. Accounts of Miracles are ſent
" from all parts: and people come from
" the moſt diſtant places, both to give ju-
" ridical teſtimony of, and to return thanks
" for their cure."

*Extract of a Letter from the Rev. Mr. Jo-
ſeph Marconi to Mr. John Baptiſt Labre,
the Father of Benedict Joſeph Labre,
dated Sept. 23, 1783.*

Speaking of the ſick perſon at Fabriano,
whom Benedict viſited and exhorted to
bear her ſickneſs with patience: he ſays.
" This ſame perſon, having, by the advice
" of her Confeſſor, invoked the Servant of
" God for three days ſucceſſively: ſhe
" each day diſtinctly heard his voice ſay-
" ing to her: *It is the will of God that you
" ſhould continue to endure your ſickneſs
" with patience.*"

A C O L-

A COLLECTION

Of divers Miraculous Cures, obtained by the Interceffion of the Venerable Servant of God, Benedict Joseph Labre : *extracted from the Regifter preferved in the Church of* S. Mary di Monti : *which in the whole amount to the Number of One Hundred and Thirty-fix : which have been certified till this Day,* July 6, 1783, *without reckoning many others, which have not yet been entered into the Regifters, on account of their not having been yet fufficiently attefted.*

April 19. Angelica Cardellini, aged twenty-four years, of the Parifh of S. Francis of Paula di Monti, having been to vifit the Corpfe of the Servant of God, by his interceffion was immediately healed of a languor, and almoft continual fever, and of a dilated vein in her breaft, which occafioned violent convulfions: and at the fame time fhe recovered her voice, which fhe had loft for the fpace of eighteen months.

On the 20th of the fame month, Angelica Raura, Widow, about Sixty Years of age, of the Parifh of S. Mark, having been brought to the Tomb of the Servant of God in a Chair, by the help of four Porters, by his interceffion recovered the ufe

of

of all her limbs, of which fhe had been deprived by two Apoplectick Fits, from which time fhe had remained unable to move herfelf on her bed for the fpace of fourteen months. She left her Chair in the Church as a memorial of her cure : and walked home to her own houfe upon her feet.

Mary Quercionnie, forty-eight years of age, daughter of Nicholas, born in the territory of Maillart, in the Marche of Ancona, in the Diocefs of Firmo, was for twenty years afflicted with a fchirrous Tumour of an extraordinary fize on her hip, with a great flow of blood, which fometimes reduced her to fuch extremity, that the laft Sacraments were adminiftred to her; being carried, on the 20th of April, to the Tomb of the Servant of God, fhe obtained a perfect cure of her fchirrous Tumour; and all her other ailments ceafed in a moment.

On the third of May, Jofeph Bonnemain of the City of Civitta-Vecchia, coming to the Tomb of the Servant of God, was immediately cured of a Fiftula in his right eye, with which he had been afflicted for the fpace of five years, and which deprived him of fight. He recovered his fight perfectly.

Qn.

On the fifth of May, Palma Sacripantie
of the City of Firmo, aged twenty years,
had a cancer in her breaft, and a continual
flux of blood, accompanied with continual
pains. She was moreover agitated with
moft violent convulfions, and vomited up
all the nourifhment fhe took. The three
laft days fhe was reduced to fuch extremity, that fhe could take nothing: was
entirely given over by the Phyficians, and
being almoft ready to breathe out her laft,
fhe invoked the Servant of God. Then
falling afleep for a moment, he appeared to
her and faid, *Arife, and eat:* which fhe
immediately did with a great appetite. After this laying down in her bed, and falling
afleep again, the Servant of God appeared
to her a fecond time, and with a diftinct
voice faid, *Arife, thou art healed.* She
then fat up, and perceived that the Cancer
which had confumed her was gone: and
with the greateft aftonifhment found that
fhe was in a ftate of fuch perfect health as
fhe had never before enjoyed.

On the ninth of May, Madam Felicia
Ruzzi, of the country of Rupitre belonging to Duke Matheo, having recourfe to
the Servant of God, and having one of his
pictures applied to her, was cured of a
chronic complaint, with which fhe had
been tormented for the fpace of eighteen
years, and which had confined her to her
bed

bed for the space of a year and a half, having her body swelled in an extraordinary manner, and being full of ulcerous wounds in her mouth and throat.

On the same day, Mrs. Rosa Lebeau, wife of Mr. Lebeau, Aide Major of the Castle of S. Angelo of the Parish beyond the Bridge, having recommended herself to the servant of God, by the application of one of his pictures, was in an instant perfectly cured of a painful swelling which she had had for the space of two years in one of her knees.

On the 10th of May, Mrs. Ann Pellevini, a Nun in a Monastery of the City of Perugia, aged twenty six years, being many years afflicted with a schirrous humour, and a continual fever, and oppressed with the Rickets, which jointly with the Schirrus had distorted her whole body, and made her right leg eight fingers breadth shorter than the left; so that she could not turn in her bed without being helped by the other Nuns, and at every time she was turned some joint or other was dislocated. Being reduced to this miserable condition, they had recourse to this good Servant of God, and by applying one of his pictures to her, she recovered a state of perfect health.

On

On the 15th of May, Dominick Falla-
vini, of the country called *The little-Poste*,
in the Manor of the Marquis of Zelloni,
made a Vow to God, that he would visit
the Tomb of Benedict. And in confequence of this Vow, setting out on his
journey: at his first departure found himself delivered from a gangrenous wound
which covered his whole leg, accompanied with exquisite pains, and which by
the Surgeons had been declared to be incurable and mortal. Scarce had he arrived at the Tomb, but he found himself
entirely cured.

On the 22d of May, Michael Goaca,
a Porter of the Parish of S. Laurence at
Ripette, having been brought in the arms
of other Porters, and laid upon the Tomb
of the Servant of God, by his interceffion,
in a moment recovered the use of all his
limbs, and likewise the use of his tongue:
and returned home to his own house without any affiftance.

On the twenty third of May, Terefa
Spoletta of the Parish of S. Nicholas-the-
Crowned, having been blind for the space
of nine years, by vifiting the Tomb of the
Servant of God, recovered her fight in an
inftant.

Sifter

Sister Mary Brunne, alias Mary du Cruz, of the Convent of S. Apollonia at Rome, being greatly wasted away by a convulsive cough, accompanied with sharp pains and a slow fever which she had had for the space of fourteen months: and being also unable to retain her food: having recommended herself to the Servant of God, and being touched with a part of one of his garments: was instantly cured: and at the same time freed from a languor to which she had been subject eighteen years.

On the twenty-fourth of May, Dominica Conty, wife of Mr. Conty, a Master Mason of the City of Baux, had been let blood in the right arm in the year 1782, by an unskilful Surgeon who in the operation wounded one of the Tendons: in consequence of which her arm was so swelled, and at the same time so contracted, that all the Faculty had resolved to proceed to amputation, as the evil had made such a progress that she could not move her joints, and her fourth finger had lost all sensation. In this condition she had recourse to the Servant of God, and when she lay down to sleep put a little bit of his linen upon her arm. In the morning when she got up, she found that she was perfectly cured.

Maria Laurentia Spadonine, forty-seven years of age, wife of Francis Tedesguini of Civitta-Vecchia, having been overturned in a cart on the 13th of September 1782, had her left arm broke, and a wound made in the right arm which cut through one of the veins and reached to the bone. Her left arm was so maimed and useless, that she could not move either her hand, or her fingers. Her right arm was likewise much maimed, though she could make some little use of it. On the 26th of May, after having prayed, and applied to her arms a small bit of the shirt of the Servant of God, she was immediately and perfectly cured.

On the twenty-seventh of May, Octavia Vergarée a native of Viterbo, living in the Square de Morganne at Rome, aged Forty-six years, having with a great deal of difficulty been carried in a Coach to the Tomb of the Servant of God, was entirely cured of a Chronoguinee which had confined her to her bed eight years.

Account

Account of a Miracle wrought through the Interceffion of the Servant of God, Bene-dict Jofeph Labre, on a Nun of the Convent of Bolene, in the Diocefs of St. Paul Trois-Chateaus: fent by M. Eymard, Archdeacon of the faid Diocefs, dated July 4, 1783.

A Nun of the Convent of the Holy Sa-crament at Bolene, a few days after her Profeffion, fell ill of a moft extraordinary complaint. For three years and a half, which her diforders have confined her to her bed, the habitual ftate of her body made her fubject to violent pains, cholicks, frequent convulfions, and faintings, fo that fhe fometimes remained as if fhe was dead; as likewife to vomitings, fpitting of blood, and an abfolute loathing of all kind of food. To thefe accumulated and conti-nued complaints, was added a great pain in her fide, which made every one fear for her life: but God referved her to make his goodnefs and his power fhine at a time when miracles appear to be fo neceffary. After each paroxifm, this good Nun was in a moft pitiful ftate; fhe frequently felt moft violent pains, which fhe faid feemed to her as if fhe had melted lead in her bowels. After about fix weeks, her con-dition grew ftill worfe: fhe voided her ex-crements by her mouth, which ordinarily

U 2   happened

happened once in two days. And they were so hard, and occasioned such violent efforts that she was almost choaked, and could scarcely pull them out with her fingers. The Physician of Bolene who constantly attended her, declares he never saw any complaint like to her's, and that if it could be in any case lawful to shorten any persons days in order to deliver them from their afflictions, it would have been lawful to have done it to this Nun, on account of her excessive sufferings.

The other Religious, who did every thing for her which Charity could suggest, performed a Novena to implore the intercession of Benedict, for her cure, and exhorted her to recommend herself to his prayers for that purpose. She replied she did not want to be cured : but only that God would give her grace to suffer with patience whatsoever he should be pleased to ordain. She persevered in these sentiments till two days before she was cured: when she began to entertain a great desire of recovering her health, that she might be able to perform the exercises prescribed by the Rule of her Order ; and above all that she might visit and adore Jesus Christ in the Blessed Sacrament.

On the twenty ninth of June, which was the last day of the Novena, this pious desire was greatly encreased ; and she expressed an earnest wish to have a picture of the

Venerable

Venerable Benedict, as she heard that some of them were in the City. She several times begged of the Nuns to procure one for her. At length they brought her one of them. Her confidence was now greater than ever : she invoked this venerable man ; and at the same time desired of the Superior that the Nuns should recommend her to God in the Vespers which they were going to say in the Choir. Behold now the wonderful work of God.

While they were saying Vespers this Nun who had lost the use of her limbs, who could scarce lift her head from her pillow, who had lost her sight through extreme weakness, and was almost at the point of death, (as has been attested by the Physician and the Religious of that house) all at once perceived herself well. *I am cured*, said she to the Infirmarian, who every moment expected her to expire : *go and fetch my habit that I may get up.* But can you see, said the Infirmarian. *Yes : very well:* said the sick person. And is not your stomach out of order ? *Look at it, said the sick person, it is come to its natural state.* The Infirmarian overjoyed, ran to fetch her habit : and at her return found her sitting upright in her bed. Being cloathed, she got upon her feet and tottered a little. Courage my dear sister, said the Infirmarian, redouble your confidence in God: and at the same time she knelt down, and cried

out

out: *My God, perfect the work you have begun.* Immediately after this, the sick person went out of the Infirmary, to go and return thanks to God. Being come to the stairs, she did not walk, but in a manner flew down. The Infirmarian being frightened screamed out. All the Community imagining that the sick person had expired, some of the Religious, and the Boarders, came immediately out of the Choir, and they met the sick Nun, who was now perfectly cured. At this instant they were beginning Complin: and that she might not interrupt the Divine Office she went to the upper Choir, to prostrate herself before the Blessed Sacrament. When Complin was finished she went down to the lower Choir, and again prostrated herself before the Blessed Sacrament, and then before her Superior. And immediately after, all the Community overjoyed, sung the *Te Deum.* I leave it to you to think what passed among these holy persons on such a marvellous occasion. After all the demonstrations of joy they offered her some Broth. *Oh !* said she, *I would rather eat for I find I have an appetite.* She eat: she assisted at the Rosary with the Community, and at supper time, went to the Refectory and eat with a good appetite. After having finished her supper, at which she eat more than any of the others, she desired to relieve the reader: and read with a strong voice; although
before

before, fhe had loft her voice. From that time fhe has every day regularly affifted at all the duties of the Community: and has always been perfectly well.

Nothing can be more falfe than the report which was fpread of her relapfe. For from the moment of her miraculous cure, fhe has without any interruption enjoyed a ftate of the moft perfect health. Her voice, her fight, her flefh, her pulfe, her ftrength was all reftored at once. She has not failed, nor does fhe fail to obferve all the Rules of the Community: being the firft at every exercife, both by day and by night, as if fhe had never been fubject to the leaft complaint.

The Phyfician of Bolene, being convinced that this cure is miraculous, intends to make his report of it to the Bifhop: who waits for his teftimony in order to tranfmit the Procefs to the Holy See.

Signed,

EYMARD,
Arch-deacon of the Diocefs of St. Paul-Trois Châteaux.

Since the publication of the French Edition of the Life of Benedict Jofeph Labre, from which this is tranflated, the following account has been received from France, viz. that " Mary Bayard, called " alfo Mary Raymond, fifty one years of " age, wife of Peter Derlate, Labourer of
" the

" the Parish of *Hefdigneul*, in the Diocefs
" of Arras, had about fifteen years ago been
" feized with a ftroke of the Palfy, from
" which time fhe was not able to move her
" leg or thigh, but they appeared as if they
" were dead, and were alfo deftitute of
" fenfation. Nor was fhe able to move her-
" felf from one place to another, but only
" by dragging herfelf upon her hands and
" knees. And for thefe laft five years her
" limbs were fo contracted that fhe was
" not able to fit upon a chair; but was
" obliged to have a particular kind of ftool
" made on purpofe for her. This poor but
" virtuous woman hoping to put an end to
" her affliction, formed a pious defign of go-
" ing to the Church of St. Sulpice de Amette,
" the Church of the place where Benedict
" was born, to implore relief from God, by
" the interceffion of his Servant. In vain
" did her friends reprefent to her, that the
" jolting of a carriage might put her in
" danger of dying on the road: for fo great
" was her confidence in the mercy of God,
" and in the powerful interceffion of his
" Servant, that fhe was refolved to fet out
" for that place. In confequence of this
" refolution, fhe on the twenty eighth of
" June 1784, received the Sacraments of
" Penance and the Euchariſt, and on the
" fame day, being accompanied by nine per-
" fons, fet out from Hefdigneul to go to
" Amette. Being arrived at the Church
                                    " Yard

" Yard of Amette, she was taken down
" from the carriage, carried into the
" Church, and placed near the Baptismal
" Font; where she remained in the most
" decent posture her situation would permit.
" Scarce had she said a few prayers, but she
" perceived a violent agitation throughout
" her whole body, and a profuse sweat
" from head to foot, but principally at
" her knees, where she also perceived
" a most violent pain which made her
" give a sudden start. Her eye-sight then
" failed her, and she almost fainted away:
" but coming to herself in a few moments
" after, she all at once raised herself up on
" her feet and cried out, *My God, I am*
" *cured: Let us return thanks to God; and*
" *acknowledge the kindness of his Servant.*
" As she had before ordered one of her
" Sons who accompanied her to light up
" some Candles in honour of Benedict
" Joseph Labre; he returned to tell her that
" he had no money left to put into the Plate
" for the Poor. *Help me,* said she, *and I*
" *will do it myself.* And accordingly she
" went, being supported by her Son. After
" which she walked round the Church, be-
" ing assisted by her two Sons, who support-
" ed her on each side holding her under
" the arms: and she walked quick, taking
" short steps like a child who is learning to
" walk. After this she went to rest herself
" at the Vicarage house, where she eat
" some

" some milk-foup, and declared all the
" abovementioned circumftances of her
" cure in prefence of a great number of the
" inhabitantsof Amette, who had affembled
" together in confequence of the report of
" this miracle : and of the perfons who had
" come with her from Hefdigneul. She
" then returned to Hefdigneul in the fame
" carriage which had conveyed her to
" Amette, where being arrived, all the
" inhabitants were aftonifhed at the news
" of her being cured. The Bells were rung,
" and a folemn *Te Deum* was fung, to re-
" turn thanks to God for fo fignal a fa-
" favour."

" The weaknefs which the faid Mary
" Helena Bayard perceived after her cure
" was the neceffary confequence of her
" formerly inactive ftate, and the poor and
" little nourifhment which fhe took. For,
" fome days after her arrival at Hefdigneul,
" having taken fome good nourifhment,
" with which fhe was fupplied by fome
" rich and pious perfons of that place, and
" of Bethune, the faid Mary Helena Bayard
" walked on foot, both to the Church, and
" to Bethune even without the help of a
" ftick : and ever fince that time has done
" the ordinary bufinefs of her ftation. She
" has alfo been vifited by feveral Phyficians
" and Surgeons who atteft her cure to be
" compleat and perfect.

" This

" This day the twenty fifth of Auguſt,
" the ſaid Mary Helena Bayard, came, ac-
" companied by ſeveral other perſons,
" from Heſdigneul to this place of Amette,
" which is near four leagues, in order to
" thank God for his mercy, and Benedict
" Joſeph Labre for his interceſſion in her
" behalf. And after having breakfaſted with
" me * with a good appetite reſted about
" two hours, and declared to me that ſhe
" does not now perceive any remains of her
" former complaint ; ſhe is now going to
" return on foot to Heſdigneul : which we
" whoſe names are hereunto ſubſcribed,
" certify to be true. In witneſs whereof
" we have hereunto ſet our hands at
" Amette this twenty fifth day of Auguſt,
" 1784."

Signed,

Playoult. *Rector of Amette.*
Bourgeois. *Vicar of Amette.*
Duhameaux. *Rector of Heſdigneul.*

N. B. The Reader is deſired to obſerve,
that though I have here related the accounts
of thoſe cures according as they have been
ſent from Rome in ſeveral letters from
ſeveral different perſons who are worthy
of

* Playoult, Rector of Amette, and one of the
Commiſſaries appointed by the Biſhop of Bou-
logne to take information concerning Benedict
Joſeph Labre.

of all credit : yet the relation of thefe facts depends only on the teftimony and veracity of the private perfons who fent thofe accounts. The Church has not yet examined and given its folemn decifion and fentence concerning any one of them. They are indeed at prefent under examination : and the greateft care will be, as it always is, taken to inveftigate the authenticity of every one in particular. So that no doubt may ever after remain of the divine interpofition in thofe which it fhall pronounce to be cures truly miraculous. This will be a work of time : becaufe feveral fteps are neceffary to be taken with each one of the cures faid to have been performed : as, 1ft. The previous exiftence of the complaint muft be proved by the teftimony of the perfon cured, of the Phyficians and others of the Faculty who attended him : and of other perfons who knew him while in his fuffering ftate.—2. The cure itfelf, or a tranfition from a ftate of infirmity to a ftate of health as likewife the permanency of the cure muft be proved by the Teftimony of the perfon cured, of Phyficians and others of the Faculty, and of other perfons who knew the perfon cured both in the ftate of ficknefs, and in a ftate of health.—3. It muft be proved, that the cure itfelf was not effected by the means of medicines or other ordinary applications, according to the prefcriptions of Phyficians or Surgeons.—4. It muft be

proved

proved that the cure was effected not in
any long tract of time, but either abfolutely or almoft inftantaneoufly, in fuch
manner as to fhew the impoffibility of its
having been effected either by art or nature.—5. It muft be proved that the inftantaneous cure or fudden tranfition
from a ftate of infirmity to a ftate of
health, was effected either in confequence
of an Invocation of the Servant of God for
that purpofe, or by the application of fomething which had formerly belonged to
him.—6. Thefe inftantaneous cures muft
be proved not only by the teftimony of
the perfons themfelves who have been
cured : but alfo by the teftimony of other
perfons who were eye-witneffes of the
mode of cure.—7. No perfons will be
admitted to give evidence to any of thefe
things, but thofe who are of mature age,
found judgment, intelligent in their profeffion of Phyfick or Surgery, and of ftrict
probity and undoubted veracity.—8. Every
thing that they teftify muft be upon
Oath.—9. And laftly, All thefe things
being committed to writing and properly
attefted by thofe who are duly authorized
to receive the depofitions of the witneffes :
muft be delivered to the Advocate of the
Faith to undergo a moft fevere fcrutiny
before the Congregation of Cardinals who
conftitute the Rota.

X   I:

It is therefore evident that the examination of these miraculous cures which are said to have been performed at the Tomb of this Servant of God and in other places will take up a confiderable time. And although they are now under examination : we have not heard that the Church has as yet pronounced its folemn fentence concerning any one of them. The only ground therefore on which they ftand at prefent, is the credit and veracity of the private though numerous witneffes who relate them as from their own knowledge and ocular demonftration. Let us not therefore prefume to forestall the judgment of the Church, by publifhing them as inconteftible miracles: but wait the event of the prefent inveftigation, not doubting but that God will according to his promife, by his Holy Spirit guide his Church into all Truth, and continue with it even to the end of the world.

MIRABILIS DEUS IN SANCTIS SUIS.

Prayers, which were daily recited by Bleſſed Benedict Joſeph Labre.

In the MORNING.

O GOD, the Creator of Heaven and Earth! my amiable Saviour! I thank Thee for the immenſe Love Thou haſt, not only for me, but for all the World! I love Thee continually above all things; and I will love Thee this Day and every Inſtant of my Life: I beſeech Thee to enable me to do thy holy Will; and I will love Thee continually for all Infidels and Sinners and will pray all this Day for them, that Thou wilt vouchſafe to enlighen them. I deſire to gain all the Indulgences I can, to deliver the poor Souls from Purgatory: finally have Mercy on Sinners and Infidels; grant me, my God, your holy Love; imprint in my Heart the Marks of your cruel Paſſion: I love you, my Jeſus, and I give you my Heart. *Amen.*

HOLY Virgin, preſerve me this Day and all the Days of my Life from all Sin, that I may not loſe the Love of my God, whom I will love for ever. I thank Thee, O holy Virgin! in the Name of all the Faithful, for the great Love thou beareſt them; and I thank Thee for all Sinners: aſſiſt them, that they may return to their amiable God; be the Refuge of all, this Day and for Ever. *Amen.*

In the EVENING.

O God of infinite Goodneſs! I moſt humbly aſk Pardon with all my Heart for all the Offences and Sins I have committed: O Lord my God! I would rather die ten thouſand Deaths than ever offend Thee, moſt Sweet Jeſus! I remit my poor Soul into thy Divine Hands; and I return Thee Thanks for thy Mercies to me this Day: I will love Thee always; may I now repoſe in the Act of pure and ſincere Love of Thee, my God. I recommend to Thee the poor Souls in Purgatory; help them and enlighten all thoſe that live in the Shades of Death, whether Infidels or Sinners. I pray to you for them; I thank you every Moment, my Divine Jeſus, for having preſerved me, that I may love you ſtill more and more; I deſire with all my Heart, to reſt in your holy Love and Grace. *Amen.*

HOLY Virgin, I thank you, with all my Heart, for all the Benefits you have procured me; I recommend to you the Souls in Purgatory: altho' I ſleep, I will love you, and thank you, in the Name of all Infidels and Sinners; help them, to the End that they may return into Favour with your Divine Son: I recommend my Soul to you and commit it into his Divine Hands. *Amen.*

THE END.

CPSIA information can be obtained
at www.ICGtesting.com
Printed in the USA
LVOW09s1752200817
545710LV00013B/121/P

9 781173 728670